HEIDEGGER AND THE QUESTION OF PSYCHOLOGY
Zollikon and Beyond

VIBS

Volume 200

Robert Ginsberg
Founding Editor

Leonidas Donskis
Executive Editor

Associate Editors

G. John M. Abbarno
George Allan
Gerhold K. Becker
Raymond Angelo Belliotti
Kenneth A. Bryson
C. Stephen Byrum
Harvey Cormier
Robert A. Delfino
Rem B. Edwards
Malcolm D. Evans
Daniel B. Gallagher
Andrew Fitz-Gibbon
Francesc Forn i Argimon
William Gay
Dane R. Gordon
J. Everet Green
Heta Aleksandra Gylling
Matti Häyry

Steven V. Hicks
Richard T. Hull
Michael Krausz
Mark Letteri
Vincent L. Luizzi
Adrianne McEvoy
Alan Milchman
Peter A. Redpath
Alan Rosenberg
Arleen L. F. Salles
John R. Shook
Eddy Souffrant
Tuija Takala
Emil Višňovský
Anne Waters
John R. Welch
Thomas Woods

a volume in
Philosophy and Psychology
PAP
Mark Letteri, Editor

HEIDEGGER AND THE QUESTION OF PSYCHOLOGY
Zollikon and Beyond

Mark Letteri

Amsterdam - New York, NY 2009

Cover photo: Dr.jur. Hans G. Müsse: View from Heidegger's vacation chalet in Todtnauberg. Heidegger wrote most of *Being and Time* there.

Cover Design: Studio Pollmann

The paper on which this book is printed meets the requirements of "ISO 9706:1994, Information and documentation - Paper for documents - Requirements for permanence".

ISBN: 978-90-420-2522-6
©Editions Rodopi B.V., Amsterdam - New York, NY 2009
Printed in the Netherlands

To JoAnne and Marie, the twin lights of my life

CONTENTS

Guest Foreword   ix
Emmy van Deurzen

Preface   xiii

Acknowledgments   xv

INTRODUCTION   1

Part One
Being in the World

ONE	Da-sein: Opening Thoughts	13
	1. Being T/here	13
	2. World and Finding	17
	3. Time and Temporality	25
TWO	Da-sein: Integral Realities	33
	1. Consciousness	33
	2. The Unconscious	34
	3. Action	40
	4. Being-with	42
	5. Bodying Forth	46

Part Two
Ways of Being

THREE	Da-sein as Possibility	55
	1. Being Called and Falling	55
	2. Being Claimed, Authenticity, and Inauthenticity	61
	3. Openness at the Limit	70
FOUR	Further Connections	
	1. Experience and Meaning	79
	2. Leaping Ahead with Da-sein	84

CONCLUSION	91
Works Cited	95
About the Author	101
Index	103

GUEST FOREWORD

Existential therapy is a search for truth. The dialogue with the client is a discussion in which we aim to elucidate and reveal life in as many guises as possible. Heidegger has contributed a tremendous amount to such explorations. His work is a much underrated resource that enables therapists and psychologists to work more deliberately and in a much more broadly based and wide ranging manner. The practice of psychotherapy and psychology as inspired by Heidegger's work is about opening up our view of the world, which is normally so closed and confined. It is about asking new ontological questions, rather than remaining based in the ontic troubles that restrain a person's being in the world. It is about getting back to fundamental truths in a person's existence so that she can build her life firmly on solid foundations.

Few psychologists and psychotherapists have gone through the trouble of studying Heidegger in any detail, in spite of the recent flourishing of the existential therapies (Cooper 2003, Cohn 2002, Deurzen 1997, Deurzen and Arnold-Baker 2005). Heidegger was one of the most important philosophers of the last century and he worked closely with Medard Boss (2001) in applying his ideas to the practice of psychiatry and psychology. These developments have left us with a wealth of guidelines on how to apply philosophy to psychotherapy and how to refocus a person's confusion by addressing those things that really matter to him.

Amongst other things Heidegger proposed that we should comprehend the far reaching consequences of the human being's (*Dasein*'s) necessary and continuing engagement with both truthful and untruthful ways of being. Dasein will always belong to its world and to some extent to other people and because of this will inevitably live in a disowned way for much of the time. Because of this Heidegger's ideas are more centered on the worldhood of Dasein and less on its internal world. He suggests that Dasein is inauthentic for most of the time, that is, taken over by the world of others, and that even when we master an authentic, owned way of being, we will inevitably return to inauthenticity again. Forgetfulness is often just a consequence of Dasein's absorption in its world and in others (Deurzen 2003). The anonymous "They" will continue to exert power over Dasein inexorably. Dasein's problem is how to be strong enough to stand up to the world in which it is embedded. To wrest itself out of its engagement with the world in order to attain a position of transcendence is a continuous challenge. Dasein can certainly achieve such transcendence momentarily in the moment of vision and with anticipatory resoluteness, but this is by no means an achievement that can be taken for granted.

In spite of Heidegger's reservations about the existence of a self, he shows how Dasein's fundamental mineness leads to its aspiration to realize its ownmost potentiality for being-itself. This mineness makes Dasein affirm its own existence as separate from anything else. This point is more clearly spelled out in *The Basic Problems of Phenomenology*:

> The Dasein exists in the manner of being-in-the-world and as such *it is for the sake of its own self.* It is not the case that this being just simply is; instead, so far as it is, it is occupied with its own capacity to be (1982, p. 170).

Dasein is preoccupied with its own Being, its own abilities and its own potential. These abilities include the ability to disclose and the ability to close off. This makes possible the idea of existing authentically (in a manner that is owned) or inauthentically (in a manner that is not owned). Authentic and inauthentic being are two sides of the same coin; they are like the day and night views of being. Both are necessary and each has a role to play. A dialectical theory of selfhood emerges, then, through an increasing awareness of one's own intentionality and choice of engagement or disengagement with the world. We learn to overcome the contradictions between authentic and inauthentic ways of being as we follow a path towards truth. As guardians of being we discover that beyond our narrow vision is a more important reality, that of the region of Being.

Of course such a radical and revolutionary way of looking at the human predicament raises difficulties for psychologists and therapists who might prefer a more clear-cut theory of normality and pathology. We will need numerous texts to help us understand and elaborate the complexity of Heidegger's thought before his ideas can be understood and absorbed into clinical practice. We need people who can translate his thinking into the everyday requirements of psychology and therapeutic practice. Then we will find that Heidegger's description of Dasein's overall struggle with existence and with its paradoxical and complementary modes of being offers us a worthwhile framework for psychotherapeutic practice.

In the present volume Mark Letteri sketches out some of these parameters with great clarity. He draws up the basic outline of a Heideggerian approach to psychology. In doing this he gives us some of the keys to access Heidegger's complex and worthwhile world and frame of reference. Psychologists and therapists have much to learn from entering this realm.

Emmy van Deurzen

References

Cohn, Hans W. (2002) *Heidegger and the Roots of Existential Therapy.* London: Continuum.

Cooper, Mick. (2003) *Existential Therapies.* London: Sage Publications.

Deurzen, Emmy van. (1997) *Everyday Mysteries: Existential Dimensions of Psychotherapy.* Oxford: Routledge.

———. (2003) *Heidegger's Enigma of Authenticity.* Ph.D. dissertation. London: City University.

Deurzen, Emmy van and Claire Arnold-Baker. (2005) *Existential Perspectives on Human Issues: A Handbook for Practice.* London: Palgrave.

Heidegger, Martin. (1982) *The Basic Problems of Phenomenology*, trans. with intro. and lexicon Albert Hofstadter. Bloomington: Indiana University Press.

———. (2001) *Zollikon Seminars: Protocols—Conversations—Letters*, ed. Medard Boss, trans. with notes and afterwords Franz Mayr and Richard Askay. Evanston, IL: Northwestern University Press.

PREFACE

Heidegger's writings often prompt puzzlement, sometimes to the point of despair. Non-philosophers in particular frequently find themselves at odds with the denseness of his language. Nonetheless, we sense in the shape of Heidegger's thinking a path that is worth exploring. In truth, he stands as one of the most important philosophers of recent times, whose influence reaches into myriad streams of intellectual and cultural life.

My aim here is to acquaint a broad readership with Heidegger's connections to psychology and related concerns, and to offer specialists one of the few monographic treatments of the topic. In pursuit of this aim, I have written this book in what I trust is an accessible and relatively non-technical way (though a few elements and sections are unavoidably technical or advanced). Keenly aware of the standard difficulties with Heidegger (whether real or perceived), I have endeavored to render the most relevant points in a limpid and succinct manner.

I hope that this book will serve as a companion to Heidegger's *Zollikon Seminars* and *Being and Time* as it concerns psychological and associated matters, so it is short. An explication and elaboration that is as lengthy (or lengthier) than the text(s) at issue might dissuade those who seek assistance, especially in the case of the putatively difficult Heidegger. For the same reason, most of the sources that I cite are standard translations from German into English or clear secondary sources that are readily available; byzantine minutia and a forbidding bibliography would impede my purposes. Readers are free to critique and refine my work here as part of the ongoing hermeneutic task of understanding Heidegger's thinking.

To avoid confusion, I employ a pair of double curly parentheses in cases in which I interpolate my own complete words into quoted material. The only exceptions are cases in which I alter only the capitalization of a single letter in a quoted word or make other minor technical adjustments. This convention is necessary owing to the liberal editorial use of square brackets in the standard translation of *The Zollikon Seminars*, a device that authors use typically to indicate their interpolations in quoted material.

ACKNOWLEDGMENTS

I owe deep thanks to Jon Mills, the former Series Editor who encouraged my efforts on this project from its earliest stages and offered me the opportunity to publish the result. I am obliged to Eric van Broekhuizen of Editions Rodopi for his support and assistance over the last few years. I am indebted to Emmy van Deurzen for her kind willingness to write the Guest Foreword. I appreciate Ernesto Spinelli's amenability in offering a supporting statement for the cover.

I am grateful to Brian MacPherson, my colleague and friend, for the innumerable formative philosophical conversations that we have shared over the years. Likewise, Jan Sobocan and Grant Yokom are steadfast allies in the life of the mind. I remember always the late Donna Foley's bountiful encouragement of my work and her personal example of a life lived well and nobly. Finally, I appreciate the enduring influence of the patient and liberal tutelage that my doctoral advisor Richard Holmes offered when I broached Heidegger's thinking many years ago.

I am beholden to my family for their sustenance throughout my many years of academic endeavors. My parents are a continuing source of affirmation. I dedicate my work here to JoAnne, my partner, and Marie, our daughter—the twin lights of my life.

INTRODUCTION

The thinking of Martin Heidegger is notoriously difficult to grasp, particularly due to its manner of expression, which is exhilaratingly innovative and frustratingly convoluted at the same time. Nonetheless, his philosophizing is powerfully important, and not just for philosophers. Psychologists and others who are concerned with understanding the essential character of human being will find in Heidegger's half a century of work a rich and penetrating collection of paths and analyses. Our task here is to articulate some aspects of his thinking well enough to form a bridge, both theoretical and practical, between his all-consuming preoccupation with being, in its intricacy and diversity, and the psychological life of human beings.

To follow the central theme of his first published work, *Being and Time*, we can say simply (for the moment) that Heidegger investigates being: what it is for something—anything at all—to be. This is ontology, a branch of metaphysics. We must add that being—*Sein*—is different from a being or beings—the region of the ontic—although not in the sense that being is a being beyond beings or that being is a merely formal and therefore empty category. Readers who are familiar with Heidegger will recognize instantly this basic concern and way of speaking. Indeed, his half a century of thinking is a mammoth, relentless, and highly adventurous attempt to answer this and only this question. The grandeur of this ontological question, however, is matched by its steepness, and its sharpness can be nearly overwhelming to those who seek in Heidegger's writings obviously accessible answers to intimately human matters. Irvin D. Yalom asserts flatly in *Existential Psychotherapy* that *Being and Time* "stands alone as the undisputed champion of linguistic obfuscation"—even while agreeing that it is "[t]he single most important philosophical text in the field" (1980, p. 16). He continues:

> The basic existential concepts themselves are not complex, they do not need to be uncoded and meticulously analyzed as much as they need to be uncovered. Every person, at some point in life, enters a "brown study" and has some traffic with existential ultimate concerns. What is required is not formal explication: the task of the philosopher, and of the therapist as well, is to de-repress, to reacquaint the individual with something he or she has known all along (p. 16).

While I take issue with some elements of Yalom's remarks, I must agree with his basic call for disclosure and recollection. Thomas Sheehan warns us in "A Paradigm Shift in Heidegger Scholarship": "In the current paradigm 'being' has become a ridiculous metaphysical caricature, so freighted with confusion and absurdity that it cannot serve as a marker for Heidegger's focal topic"

(2001, p. 189). Heidegger strives to curb misunderstandings by forcing his readers, using extraordinary means, to abandon their preconceptions of "the matter of thinking": "In 1955 he resorted to crossing out the word *Sein* so as to emphasize the distance between 'being' {{understood in a merely traditional sense}} and his own topic" (p. 189). Sheehan also criticizes the translation of *Dasein*—Heidegger's word for the human being—as "being there": "One of the least happy moves of Heidegger-scholarship has been to translate the *Da* of *Da-sein* as 'there.' But with Heidegger's *Da*, . . . there is no there there" (p. 193). This book employs both the terms "being" and "there," though in a way (the reader can hope) that is consistent with Sheehan's call to understand Heidegger's "focal topic" as "de-hypostatized openness" (p. 200). We must avoid the trap of "first positing the ontological difference between being and entities and then opting for the 'being'-side" (p. 188).

Whatever its complexity, Heidegger's thinking contains a salient, engaging, and ineradicable focus on human being that, engaged carefully, yields deep accomplishment. Published in 1927, *Being and Time* is his most familiar work, and its so-called existentialist slant makes it the most obvious point of departure for any effort to gain clarity about the nature of human being. Heidegger continues to explore searchingly this fundamental question in his other works, albeit in different and sometimes seemingly disparate manners. The so-called "turn" in his thinking in the 1930s leads not to an utterly different sort of human being but to one who still bears the marks of Da-sein—the human being—of *Being and Time*. Our task is to sift through the various expressions of human being in Heidegger's philosophical ruminations to discover the ones that are elemental. We can hope that the result will be a faithful, substantial, and concretely meaningful approach to the human being, one that grounds and enriches the psy-chologies which presume to hold the key to our existence. Heidegger states in *Zollikon Seminars*: "The unifying pole in all psychotherapeutical science is the existing human being" (2001, p. 207). We should take this declaration as a promise.

We must avoid the danger of construing Heidegger simply as an "existentialist," since this term bears a plethora of connotations, some of which we may find unhelpful or even unappealing. For instance, we may sense that existentialism is a philosophical approach which glorifies the arbitrariness of personal choice and indulges the drama of subjective experience. Any faithful and charitable reading of his work should demonstrate the shallowness or outright falseness of such an interpretation. We might call various approaches existentialist. For example, Søren Kierkegaard emphasizes the solitary mortal choosing the hard road toward God, Friedrich Nietzsche the destructive creator of vital values, Jean-Paul Sartre the subject struggling grimly to accept responsibility, and Simone de Beauvoir the individual joining with others in devotion to freedom. Heidegger concerns himself—sometimes for different reasons—with many of the same topics. He departs, however, from the stereotypical existentialist and humanistic preoccupation with "the subject." In any event, Heidegger, writing in the golden age of existentialism as a popular perspective, claims starkly that philosophy has come to its logical end in the form of Nietzsche, the "last metaphysician," so it is impossible to ignore the subversively radical character of his probing.

The term existentialism is nevertheless important historically, and we can use it to gain clarity about particular aspects of Heidegger's thinking. We should not use it, however, as an easy label for his undertaking, even if it appears to afford an obvious point of contact for those who seek the "psychological" Heidegger. Readers who are unfamiliar with him except for his reputation as a so-called existentialist should understand from the outset that his efforts involve but move far beyond a basic emphasis on the "choosing human being." Heidegger's thinking offers much to psychologists, psychotherapists, and counselors, but cannot be reduced at all to the once or twice removed smatterings in psychological literature with which many are familiar (especially in the context of humanistic psychology). Even the Swiss psychiatrist Ludwig Binswanger's earnest pioneering move in the early 1930s to adapt *Being and Time* falls short of full advantage, on Heidegger's view. Roger Frie, a contemporary Binswangerian, argues the merits of Binswanger's approach, *contra* Heidegger, in *Understanding Experience*; Joseph J. Kockelmans, on the other hand, avers in "Reflections on the 'Foundations' of Psychology and Psychoanalysis" that Binswanger perpetuated metaphysical problems inasmuch as he "continued to speak of description, essence, idea, and consciousness" (1995, p. 538). The Heideggerian look at the human condition solicits and challenges our usual sense of our being in the world, not just our intellect. As such, it is a call to transformation of our whole being, fraught with intractable questions and uncanny insights. Simply expressed, this transformation is real work. Whatever the ultimate nature or outcome of Heidegger's task, it is not easy. This is fitting.

Heidegger reached out to the world of psychology and psychiatry by holding seminars for psychiatry students. The Swiss psychiatrist and psychoanalyst Medard Boss attests in "Martin Heidegger's Zollikon Seminars" that Heidegger

> confided in me that he had hoped that through me—a physician and psychotherapist—his thinking would escape the confines of the philosopher's study and become of benefit to wider circles, in particular to a large number of suffering human beings (1978–1979, p. 7).

As a result, as Keith Hoeller reports, "for seventeen years Heidegger traveled to Switzerland to give seminars to Boss's medical students, professors, and therapists" (1978–1979, p. 4). Boss indicates that Heidegger's first seminars "led often to the fantasy that a Mars man had encountered a group of Earth dwellers for the first time and was trying to communicate with them" (1978–1979, p. 10). He scarcely overstates the point; Heidegger's efforts to stimulate his scientific auditors ran noticeably contrary to their traditional training and even everyday ways of thinking. Indeed, many of his ruminations—which he intends in this context as relatively down to earth—are difficult to follow even for those who are familiar with philosophical discourse. Notwithstanding the sometimes daunting quality of Heidegger's speculations, we must pay due attention to the published form of these protocols, *Zollikon Seminars*, in our sustained attempt to link Heidegger's thinking and both the theory and practice of "psy" endeavors. The *Seminars* comprise the most explicit and determined attempt by Heidegger to make connections with psychology, and we can decipher this text if we prepare adequately a preliminary account of his orientation.

Despite the initial difficulty with the seminars, which they inaugurated in the 1950s, Heidegger and Boss managed to cultivate a rich application of Heideggerian philosophy to psychotherapy known as Daseinsanalysis. This psychotherapeutic approach continues today, with formal training headquarters in Switzerland. Much more prevalent, however, is Heidegger's general influence that appears broadly across phenomenological, existential, and humanistic psychology. While Karl Jaspers, the German psychiatrist and philosopher, developed an approach just prior to *Being and Time* that some view as existentialist, Heidegger is much more prominent as a modern philosopher of human existence—even though Jaspers's unabashedly humanistic slant might be more palatable to the average person than Heidegger's ontological preoccupation. Heidegger's unique analyses of the lived world of self and others, choice and responsibility, authenticity and inauthenticity, and death surely possess a haunting power, which explains their longevity. He manages to join together elements of the reflections of Aristotle and medieval philosophers (ontology), Kierkegaard ("existence"), Nietzsche ("life"), and Edmund Husserl (phenomenology), creating a potent context through which to explore the human condition. Heidegger aims to understand our human reality from the "inside" through to the "outside"—not in a merely subjectivistic manner, but with an eye to our essential place in the greater unfolding of the universe. His work, therefore, is a treasure for those are passionate about the human but who also see the need to steer clear of narcissism. For the same reason it also stands opposed to most postmodern tendencies: Heidegger's "meditative thinking" seeks truth, while postmodernism generally seeks nothing. Jon Mills speaks of "how reductionistic versions of postmodernism delude themselves into thinking that there is no individuality or teleology of conscious agency," arguing that "this claim is absurd: I exist by virtue of the fact that I posit myself and contemplate my thoughts, feelings, and actions through determinate choice and action" (2003, p. 134). Heidegger might not argue the case using quite the same language, but the sentiment is the same: We exist, and our existence is a truth. While a hermeneutic or interpretive thinker of language, Heidegger refuses to construe the human being as an "epiphenomenon of larger cultural and linguistic forces" and instead acknowledges and respects the "subject who emerges within them equiprimordially" (p. 135). M. Guy Thompson says in "Postmodernism and Psychoanalysis: A Heideggerian Critique of Postmodern Malaise and The Question of Authenticity":

> Though Heidegger was instrumental in our era's recognition of the illusory nature of the self {{in comparison with current or traditional reifications}}, he argued that because the self is impressionable it is imperative to find a way home, without selling ourselves short (2004, p. 186).

Heidegger's search for truth is hardly naïve or uninformed. For those who are willing to take seriously the orbit of his thinking, the rewards are great.

Heidegger's views on science (and scientism) are particularly important in the present context. Those who interpret psyche and action by way of the natural sciences or even the more ostensibly accommodating social sciences will find his thinking a demanding yet decidedly ascientific undertaking. We must not take ascientific to mean unrigorous, for Heidegger pursues with extraordinary care a better understanding of humankind and cosmos. Instead, in keeping with his teacher Husserl's constant exhortation (for example, in *The Crisis of European Sciences and Transcendental Phenomenology*), he refuses to accept the approaches of the sciences—their "regional ontologies"—as givens. Heidegger's project cannot proceed on the basis of untested method-related and ontological assumptions, as he indicates plainly in the *Seminars*: "Nowadays, human beings reject the importance of things experienced directly. They do not count. Meanwhile, most proofs rest on mere hypotheses" (2001, p. 215). In the final analysis, his thinking of being touches a deeper level of reality than the sciences can reach on their own, limited as they are by their own historically determined and indeed occluded points of origin. We should not demur on account of Heidegger's criticisms of science; the fact that he attempted to engage scientists (Boss's psychiatry students) evinces his belief in (or at least his strong hope for) dialogical success in this respect.

In the very first line of the *Seminars* Heidegger states unequivocally that "human existing in its essential ground is never just an object which is present-at-hand; it is certainly not a self-contained object" (p. 3). This much is clear from *Being and Time* as well. He goes on to characterize "human existing" as "'pure,' invisible, intangible capabilities for receiving-perceiving [*Vernehmen*]" (p. 4). The first three expressions are undoubtedly alien to scientific ears. Heidegger then asserts more strongly: "[A]ll conventional, objectifying representations of a capsule-like psyche, subject, person, ego, or consciousness in psychology and psychopathology must be abandoned in favor of an entirely different understanding" (p. 4). The opposite of "capsule-like" is (perhaps we can say) "open textured," or, as he says, receiving-perceiving. Receiving-perceiving suggests a responsive organism, and here Heidegger seems to come close to the biological-scientific perspective of his seminar participants. For instance, he says: "The human being cannot be subdivided into parts, one that is a part of nature and the other, the more central one, that is not a part of nature" (p. 28). Indeed, much of the thinking in the *Seminars* is devoted to exploring the "bodying forth" of Da-sein. Nonetheless, Heidegger hastens to add that Da-sein "is not something which can be objectified at all under any circumstances" (p. 4). Instead, "to exist as Da-sein means to hold open a domain through its capacity to receive-perceive the significance of the things that are given to it and that address it by virtue of its own 'clearing'" (p. 4). These are not categories by which natural scientists or even social scientists usually interpret human existing. Is this an eccentric philosophical orientation that purports to extend itself to the scientific mind but which in fact resists utterly any scientific endeavor to understand human being?

Heidegger does not (and cannot coherently) deny the reality of the manifold things or objects that we perceive. His concern, however, is our nature as those who *encounter* things or objects. Our nature as receiving-perceiving beings—though described as "invisible" and "intangible"—is more primordial than such overt things or objects, which could not otherwise be what they are for us. Of course, the "for" here presupposes the hermeneutic or interpretive circle of understanding. An unencountered world could not be a human world. Being t/here as encountering takes in what is given, and what is given could not be such in the absence of this reception. On Heidegger's view, things or objects are real in the common physical sense, but can have no meaning for us except through our nature as understanding beings. A human world of things cannot stand apart from our receiving-perceiving. Readers who are familiar with *Being and Time* already know Heidegger's signature criticism of atomistic views of the human being. Borrowing from Maurice Merleau-Ponty, we can ask: What is the relation between the visible and the invisible? Da-sein's essential character is the key. Heidegger says in the *Seminars*: "Before we can perceive a table as this or that table, we must receive-perceive that there is something presencing [*Anwesen*]"; therefore, "[o]ntological phenomena, . . . are primary [in the order of being], but secondary in [the order of] being thought and seen" (p. 6). The "nonsensory, imperceptible" ontological fact of the existence of a table is "*prior to* all perceptible phenomena" (p. 6). Richard Holmes says in *The Transcendence of the World: Phenomenological Studies*: "I may doubt whether a particular being is or is not, but in order for that doubt to arise, I must already see that what-is 'is' in the world; the world is the pool or field of Being" (1995, p. 46). Even more strongly, Heideggerian truth is a-letheia: un/covering, in which concealment or withdrawing is as essential as unconcealment or showing. Lest we find ourselves frightened away by Heidegger's unusual approach, especially if we are natural or social scientists, we should ponder the sober logic of Heidegger's point and the human promise of a way of thinking that respects the distinctiveness of our basic situation. While eschewing solipsism and narcissism, he accords extraordinarily concentrated reflection to the question of what it is to be human. As Heidegger fulfills Husserl's directive to be faithful to the phenomena, so we should hold fast to the matter of thinking—Sheehan's "de-hypostatized openness"—wherever it leads us.

In discussing the subject of time in the *Seminars* Heidegger says explicitly that we must "disregard" psychological and scientific approaches in favor of the "*phenomenological* way of thinking" (2001, p. 59). He says that phenomenology "deals with what is prior to all conceptualization and {{merely}} subjective, emotional experiencing" (p. 131). By way of background, Heidegger maintains that the reality and meaning of the most primitive assumptions in science are largely unthought. (Such a claim requires much explanation and defense, of course.) Given the prevalence of scientific pursuits in the contemporary world, this paucity of reflection is highly important, and so we must uncover these origins. In uncovering these fundamental suppositions, Heidegger believes that we will come to see more clearly the ontologically vital core which informs all aspects of our being—including the psyche and body as objects of technical scrutiny. After all, as he says: "The art of interpretation is the art of asking the right questions" (p. 54). Heidegger warns of the danger of hastiness in thinking: "The human being's being-open to being is so fundamental and decisive in being human that, due to its inconspicuousness and plainness, one can continuously overlook it in favor of contrived psychological theories" (p. 74). Thinking about our dwelling as human beings, here called a sojourn or *Aufenhalt* (p. 87), demands a sort of simplicity that is often difficult to achieve for many reasons. As Boss says in "Recent Considerations in Daseinsanalysis", "the whole of daseinsanalysis, what Heidegger's teaching has taught me" is "only to open my eyes":

> And also this is the whole direction that phenomenology or daseinsanalysis can give to a patient: to help him to open his eyes and to look at the things themselves and not to build theories beforehand and then to look through the theories to the human being (1988, p. 41).

We need to keep in mind this fundamental idea for the duration of our exploration.

Heidegger's ruminations in the *Seminars* about the *logos* or "logic" of *psyche* or "mind" begin with general thoughts about science's assumptions and move rather quickly to questions of calculability and then *soma* or body. ("The Question Concerning Technology"—a much earlier piece—is premised on the question of calculability.) As psychiatry students, his auditors were trained physicians and thus oriented essentially toward the body as a physical object that is amenable to inspection and manipulation. Speaking of the alleged or desired measurability of the relation between *psyche* and *soma*, Heidegger states: "But this is an unjustified claim, because it has not been derived from the subject matter in question, but from the [following] scientific claim and dogma: Only what is measurable is real" (2001, p. 80). More strongly, science, because of its assumptions, tends to reduce phenomena to what is measurable. Science thus tends to reduce *psyche* to *soma*. Such a reduction deforms our understanding not only of *psyche* but *soma* as well. Indeed, Heidegger claims, "Da-sein is not spatial because it is embodied. But its bodiliness is possible only because Da-sein is spatial in the sense of making room" (p. 81). "Making room" is not a physical concept, yet it is faithful phenomenologically to our actual experience as human beings. Heidegger insists on analyzing human existing by way of what is essential, where the essential is what claims human existing in the most original way, whether or not this corresponds with conventional attitudes, scientific or otherwise. Kockelmans says:

> The philosophical analytic of *Dasein* offers the possibility of understanding man both as part of nature {{the biological view}} and as a "part" of culture with its tradition and heritage {{the anthropological view}}; it offers equally the possibility of understanding man as transcendence. This way the separation of mind, soul, and spirit can be obviated, without us having to declare their distinction to be meaningless (1995, p. 537).

The same holds true for Da-sein as a being who always and already lives an (as) embodied existence: "[A]ll forms of ex-isting and all forms of comportment are necessarily bodily" (p. 540).

Heidegger's emphasis in the *Seminars* on *soma* is certainly welcome in itself, as *Being and Time* does not include such a treatment. Later thinkers such as Merleau-Ponty and Sartre offer philosophies of embodiment that are inspired by him (among others). Moreover, Heidegger's gambit is to seize upon his medical auditors' central absorption with the body as a way of enticing them to listen to the address of "the open" in/of human existing. For example, Da-sein's reality as a spatial being leads us to think of "making room" as a phenomenon of human existing, which in turn suggests that Da-sein dwells in a "clearing" which is primordial ontologically. The idea of a clearing in this sense is hardly scientifically measurable or verifiable. While there may be no way to create a conventionally scientific or social scientific operational definition of this concept, we can on Heideggerian terms "operationalize" the thought of a clearing that grants us the making of room and thus spatiality. Daseinsanalysis is one example of such an (intended) "operationalization" (rendered in quotes on account of Heidegger's critique of objectification and mere technique). Science is an undertaking that presupposes our elemental condition as beings who always and already exist concernfully in a world of persons and things: "One must see that science as such (i.e., all theoretical-scientific knowledge) is founded as a way of being-in-the-world—founded in the bodily having of a world" (2001, p. 94).

Heidegger rejects the criticism that he is anti-scientific: "[I]t is not a matter of hostility toward science as such, but a matter of critique regarding the prevailing lack of reflection on itself by science" (p. 95). For instance, he asks, what should we make of the expression, "I am all ears"? (p. 96). We might well wonder what such an expression could tell us about the nature of the human being, let alone what natural or social scientific status it might hold or promise. "Being all ears" assumes ears, naturally, but also bodiliness in a broader sense, environmental orientation, motility—and a concern to listen to specific words (rather than merely receive passively the results of one's sensory registers). As Heidegger concludes: "Hearing and speaking, and thus language in general, are *also* always phenomena of the body. Hearing is a being-with-the-theme in a bodily way.... Bodying forth [*Leiben*] always belongs to being-in-the-world" (pp. 96–97). His vision of human existing is clearly holistic and relational, which explains why he takes great pains to demonstrate the one-sidedness and ultimate inadequacy of strictly scientific approaches to understanding ourselves. Again, Heidegger's approach is rigorous, but in a phenomenologically pure manner. The body is the object of science, but it is true as well and in a deeper sense that we exist as bodying forth, a reality that is not amenable to measurement. What, then, of science and the question of measurement? Heidegger affirms: "Measurability means calculability.... But calculability means *precalculability*. And this is decisive because the point is *control* and *domination*" (pp. 104–105). At this juncture, though, we must desist from elaborating on his claim, as doing so would take us far afield. Let us say simply that Heidegger interprets our basic character as human beings with passionate respect for "the open" by virtue of which we are as we are, a reality that defies any undemanding or mercenary construal. The intent of this book is to highlight and explore primary themes in Heidegger's thinking with the aim of inspiring beneficial vantages on the assorted "psy" endeavors. The intent is not to deduce a fixed psychological theory or apparatus. Darren Wolf in "Heidegger's Conscience" avers that "it {{is not}} appropriate to try and 'understand' the client along the lines of Heidegger's philosophical structure" if this means "curtailing the possibilities of Dasein" (1999, p. 60). Instead, the point is to "take up a relationship with his method and text," which is "the therapeutic in Heidegger's philosophy" (p. 61). "Life is always already philosophical," Wolf says, and in "Everything You Ever Wanted to Know About Heidegger (But Were Afraid to Ask Your Therapist)" he cautions us against the danger of "the settled": "Tradition takes what we are left by former generations, by institutions, by colleagues and makes it {{what we believe we know}} seem obvious; it makes us forget to ask questions" (2000, p. 58). "[Q]uestioning," as Heidegger says in the last line of "The Question Concerning Technology", is "the piety of thought" (1977b, p. 35). His contemporary mission accords with the vision of the ancient philosophers as expressed by Pierre Hadot in *Philosophy as a Way of Life*: "[P]hilosophy was a mode of existing-in-the-world, which had to be practiced at each instant, and the goal of which was to transform the whole of the individual's life" (1995, p. 265).

Part One

BEING IN THE WORLD

One

DA-SEIN: OPENING THOUGHTS

1. Being T/here

Those who are familiar with Heidegger's thinking already know his famous anti-Cartesian (or, perhaps more accurately, extra-Cartesian) position, especially as articulated in such a groundbreaking manner in *Being and Time*. While a lengthy treatment of this theme is unnecessary (and would be utterly unoriginal), a recapitulation is required to prepare the way for the more detailed analyses of self, other, and sojourning that follow.

Heidegger calls the fundamental feature of human existing "being in the world"—"Being-in-the-world in general as the basic state of Dasein," as one of the headings runs in *Being and Time* (1962, p. 78). We should resolve this term into its elements: being, in, and world. We say of being: Being is. While this may sound like a joke to the uninitiated, it most certainly is not for Heidegger. His entire philosophical career hinges on this matter of thinking as explored and expressed in a number of ways. Heidegger investigates being: what it is for something—anything at all—to be. Being is not merely a being or beings, although it is also not something beyond beings or a merely formal and therefore empty category. He endeavors to "say" being, and in *Being and Time* and throughout his corpus he does so, in the final analysis, by way of the human sort of being. Everything (anything) that is, is by virtue of being. Everything (anything) that is, "has" being. Do we understand what this means? Heidegger answers affirmatively: We understand being to the extent that *we* are a kind of being—a uniquely interrogative being, he believes. We possess, or, more accurately, live out a comprehension of self, others, and mortal dwelling—in other words, a comprehension of our being human. Furthermore, as human beings, we always and already dwell in a world that is full of other human beings, things, practical facts, and contingencies. Our peculiar embeddedness, our "in-ness," distinguishes us immediately from non-human beings such as stones that are in the world in a categorially different way. As a being of possibilities, a human being is not an object. Stones change, but they have no possibilities. Their changeability evinces no inherent purpose, no authorship. Our "in-ness" is meaningfully kinetic. Finally, our world is not set apart as the world of Descartes in the *Meditations* stands over and truly against the (putatively) human type of being. Instead, our world—the world in which we find ourselves, others, and things, and in and through which we appropriate the possibilities that give substance to our lives—is who we are. We are our world. Heidegger says in the *Seminars* that "being-in-the-world itself . . . is not composed of components, although in its unity it can be brought into one's interpretive view according to its different aspects" (2001, p. 138).

We must consider the origin of the word Da-sein. In German, the *Da* element means there, while the *sein* element means being. The straightforward translation is there-being, or, more eloquently, being-there. This way of speaking shows the eventful nature of human being: We appear and dwell in the open region of world. We must exist in some particular place at some particular time: "There" means that we stand out in the world as distinctive localized beings. The word there also contains the word here, and part of the truth of our being is the fact that we always and already exist here (and now) in our own world. We could say: Human beings "appear there" or emerge in the world in the midst of beings and "dwell here" in a world of meanings and projects. Thus, we may more mindfully write being-there as being t/here, without fear of linguistic excess. "Being t/here" characterizes the formal structure of Da-sein's existence. Furthermore, we always and already dwell meaningfully with others in the "here" of our world, a reality to which Heidegger applies the term being-with. This, too, is coeval.

As the "there" of being t/here, Da-sein is thrown into existence, pro-jected into a sphere over which it has only partial control. This thrownness is the factical aspect of Da-sein's existence: its being-thrown into enworldedness. Heidegger does not use the word factual, as it implies object-ive, or objectifying, realism, a crudity for which he lacks patience: "A fact [*Tatsache*] is something real, but it is not reality. Reality is not a fact, otherwise it would be something ascertainable like a mouse beside something else" (2001, p. 154). As a factical being, Da-sein did not ask to be born, but it was born all the same. It did not ask to be born male or female, but it was born male or female all the same. Da-sein did not ask to be born in this place or at that time, but it was born in this place or at that time all the same. It did not ask to be born into these circumstances or those circumstances, but it was born into a determinate set of conditions all the same. These states of affairs form the elemental facticity of Da-sein's being in the world, a truth with which it must grapple ceaselessly. Sheehan says: "[H]uman beings are the *Da* {{the open}} not occasionally or by their own choice, but of necessity. We cannot *not* be the open (the possibility of taking-as) . . ." (2001, p. 194). While facticity or thrownness shapes the human condition, Da-sein is more than a being who is merely thrown into circumstances—it is a "throwing" being who lives meaningfully in and through past, present, and future. As Jonathan Hall says in "Understanding and Interpretation in the Clinical Setting: A Heideggerian Perspective":

> This {{freedom and responsibility}} means being able to experience Being-in-the-world not as a mere set of "circumstances" which are subsumed under universally valid principles {{"objectivity"}}, but as a

"Situation" where the choice demanded of us is defined by the concrete characteristics of the context itself (2004, p. 112).

Edwin L. Hersch says in *From Philosophy to Psychotherapy: A Phenomenological Model for Psychology, Psychiatry, and Psychoanalysis*:

> The particular truth elaborated will always be incomplete, since it is limited by the particular perspective of the person experiencing it (spatially, temporally, culturally, ideationally, motivationally, emotionally, historically, etc.), as well as by the particular aspects or properties of the object, which are more or less hidden in that particular relational experience. But neither will it be arbitrary, purely voluntary, or mere projection, since the "unyieldingness" of Reality also contributes to our experiences (2003, p. 70).

The human being is an active reality who pro-jects herself into a factically conditioned yet humanly understood and interpreted world of purposes and plans that span the three dimensions or "ek-stases" of time. As the "here" of being t/here, Da-sein shapes the world of its concern: itself, others, and things. It is a throwing thrownness: a pro-jecting pro-jection, a kinetic opening. As enworlded, as an active being, Da-sein always and already articulates understandings and interpretations. We are "saying" beings. These articulations are not supplemental additions to Da-sein's being in the world, but part of the fabric of its unique manner of being.

The condition of Da-sein is such that it dwells in a region of intelligibility—its world is infused with a sense of coherence and bearing. Coherence may disintegrate and bearing may falter—things may go wrong—but this condition always holds sway in the first instance. (A problem or dearth presupposes a preferred path, an orientation of some sort.) "In the first instance" means that Da-sein is (must be) always and already here . . . as a being who stands out . . . and moves this way or that to reach . . . . Da-sein's sayings (its uses of language) embody its distinctive manner of being as it lives concretely, in multiple ways, this manner of being. Da-sein as a throwing thrownness who articulates meanings is thus a being who is concerned with its world. Tim LeBon says in *Wise Therapy: Philosophy for Counsellors*:

> Meaning as purpose refers specifically to someone's conscious intentions {{an explicit determination to accept or reject *x*}} . . . ; meaning as significance can take a much broader perspective {{a sense of the import of an action or event or reality apart from our particular designs}} . . . . Questions about the meaning of life seem to be about both—we are interested in both the purpose and significance of life (2001, p. 129).

Da-sein is a being of care, to use the standard translation of Heidegger's German word *Sorge*. Hans W. Cohn prefers the term "involvement" (1997, p. 125). As an engaged or involved being, Da-sein is care-ful. It lives concernfully in its world: Da-sein's movements matter, else it would not undertake them. Heidegger says in the *Seminars* that "human Da-sein (being-there) is *sojourning [sich aufhalten] in the clearing* and 'concerns itself with' [*beschäftigt mit*] things" (2001, p. 144). As we will see shortly, even boredom, which appears to be proof of the possibility of a total lack of concern, serves to reveal the concerned or engaged character of the human condition. Heidegger gives the "existential formula for the structure of care as 'ahead-of-itself—Being-already-in (a world) as Being-alongside (entities encountered within-the-world)'" (1962, p. 364). Da-sein did not ask to be born—but given that Da-sein has been born, it finds itself claimed:

> The human being could not live without this being addressed. "Stress" is something that preserves "life" in the sense of this necessity of being addressed.... [T]his being burdened—the stress—belongs to the essential constitution of the human being (2001, p. 137).

An address calls for a response; thus "we are conversation" (p. 140). Heidegger observes that "our *being-in-the-world* always already fundamentally {{consists}} of a receptive/perceptive relatedness to something which addresses us from out of the openness of our world, from out of that openness as which we exist" (p. 232). Da-sein is thus characterized by "*direction*" (p. 232). He says of the "essence" of our identity: "The constancy [*Ständigkeit*] of the self is proper to itself in the sense that the self is always able to come back to itself and always finds itself still the same in its sojourn [*Aufenthalt*]" (p. 175). This constancy is not a substance, as substances are "present-at-hand within the course of time", that is, they are objects contained in time as a holder (p. 175). Instead, as care-ful beings we *are* temporally, and our world, even filled as it is with the physical, is at root a world of ecstatic pro-jection: "Receiving-perceiving means much more than merely sensory, optical seeing. We receive-perceive exactly what is essential here without seeing it in a sensory fashion with the eyes" (p. 35). Heidegger takes extraordinary trouble throughout his career to distinguish the human being as receiving-perceiving being-in-the-world from the human being as a thing:

> As to the physician's will-to-help [the patient]: One must pay attention to the fact that it involves a *way of existing* and not the *functioning* of something. If one only aims at the latter, then one does not add to [the understanding] of Da-sein. But this is the goal. (p. 157; emphases added).

The aspiration is to understand Da-sein, which means that we seek a hermeneutic deepening of the understanding of ourselves that we always and already "have" and live—that we are. We seek to deepen ourselves. As Hall says: "Understanding, for Heidegger, is not something we aim at {{abstractly}}, it is what we do" (2004, p. 111). Likewise, Ran Lahav remarks in "A Conceptual Framework for Philosophical Counseling: Worldview Interpretation": "Life consists of a continuous interpretation of ourselves and the world. Philosophical counseling offers a controlled and directed environment in which life—herein understood as a process of interpretation—is intensified" (1995, p. 24).

2. World and Finding

Being and Time is an ample and incisive attempt to understand Da-sein's enworlded character. What does dwelling in a world mean? In the *Seminars*, Heidegger distinguishes world and environment: "Linguistic usage, according to which one speaks of human and animal 'behavior' indiscriminately, does not take into account the unfathomable, essential difference between the relationship to a 'world' [*Weltbezug*] and to an 'environment' [*Umgebungsbezug*]" (2001, p. 244). Animals experience an environment, while human beings experience a world of meaning: a chosen and articulated gathering together of possibilities in a pressing forward. Heidegger says that we consider animals *as* animals inasmuch as "we humans as ek-sistent {{surpassing beings}} have *engaged in advance in* [*eingelassen*] the relationship to the environment proper to the animal" (p. 244). We need not—cannot—experience the animal's environment exactly as the animal does; the point is that we have a pro-jective understanding—a pre-apprehension—of the animal's type of being, a grasp that recognizes but exceeds the animal's manner of being. Da-sein as being t/here exists in a world into which it has been thrown but in which it, too, "throws" possibilities. Its world is suffused with a kind of active and complex meaning that does not appear in animal life. While the animal lives in an environment, it has no comprehension of its relation to its environment *as* environment, Heidegger claims. Da-sein, however, experiences and articulates its world as world (as meta-environment), even if this lived reality happens not to be expressly reflective in everyday life. We can here employ the well-known phenomenological-existentialist concepts of *Umwelt*, *Mitwelt*, and *Eigenwelt*. *Umwelt* denotes "having an environment", and animals certainly have an environment (1962, p. 84). The "aroundness" of the physical environment for Da-sein, Heidegger explains, is "founded upon the worldhood of the world": Its particular lived reality is rooted in Da-sein's broader truth of moving perpetually in a world of concern beyond the obviously physical (p. 135). *Mitwelt* denotes the "with-world" of Da-sein as a being in the world who dwells always in the company of others. *Eigenwelt* or "own-world" denotes what we may call simply individuated existence. These three "worlds" constitute the *being-in* of Da-sein as being-in-the-world. We exist with things around us, with others, and with ourselves. The instances of with-ness here presuppose the hermeneutic circle of interpretation: the originative reality of taking something as . . . in all our dealings. World is not a thing (or set of things), a container, or a coldly objective entity "out there"; it is the full manner in which Da-sein moves concernfully. Hersch offers: "[W]e should really be talking here of a hermeneutic 'spiral' rather than a hermeneutic 'circle,' since the place to which we return is never quite the same one and the spiral figure implies a progression in a particular direction" (p. 169). Heidegger says:

> As understanding, Dasein projects its Being upon possibilities. . . . The projecting of the understanding has its own possibility—that of developing itself . . . . This development of the understanding we call "interpretation". In it the understanding appropriates understandingly that which is understood by it. In interpretation, understanding does not become something different. It becomes itself (1962, p. 188).

Heidegger distinguishes famously using the example of a hammer the "ready-to-hand" and the "present-at-hand." In the first instance, the reality of a hammer rests in its usefulness for our purposes, its intimate place in the sway of our concerns. It is ready-to-hand for our designs. Only when the hammer breaks and we stare at the now useless assemblage of components do we view the hammer from a distance as an "object": as a bare thing that is (merely) present-to-hand. So the world is not "the" world (somewhere out there); it is always and already *our* world. Sheehan says: "Being/sense is neither 'out there' in entities nor 'in here' in our heads" (2001, p. 192). As Cohn asserts simply in "Why Heidegger?": "[T]here is no world without human beings, and human beings cannot be defined outside a world" (1999, p. 8). Sheehan argues: "[I]n Heidegger's phenomenological perspective *est* {{"is"}} never appears alone but always in conjunction with an *Entwurf des Seins*, an act of 'taking-something-as'"—"to make sense of it" (2001, p. 189, p. 190). Thus, "presence is always the current *sense* that things have in relation to, and within the world of, human concerns" (p. 191). Sheehan speaks of "thrown-openness-as-ability-to-make-sense-of" (p. 195). Da-sein's world of "sense-making relations" makes things "intelligible-as" (p. 193). This ability "[t]o 'clear' something means to free it from dumb lethic {{opaque}} 'thereness' by relating it to human purposes" (p. 193).

> . . . Heidegger agrees that we do enjoy a categorical intuition of "is," but that is hardly a blinding insight into Being-As-Such. Rather, categorical intuition is our immediate presence to mediation, to the inevitability of taking-as and making-sense-of . . . . The categorical intuition does not deliver an all-at-once vision of Big Being but is about our thrownness into

the "as," our ineluctable discursivity. That is why Heidegger prefers to call it "hermeneutical intuition" (p. 192).

Da-sein's being "in" the world is being *as* world. On Sheehan's account, Heidegger's "matter of thinking" is *"what makes possible* any 'as' or 'is'" (p. 192).

Many commentators have referred, at least traditionally, to Da-sein's original state of awareness as "mood." Heidegger spends many pages in *Being and Time* examining what we might call mood, but he takes pains at every point to distinguish his conception of mood from unhelpful or distracting senses. Heidegger speaks of *Stimmung*, or mood, and *Befindlichkeit*, or "situatedness." The English terms mood and situatedness, however, do not capture his full intent. Mood suggests, rightly, a basic orientation. Situatedness suggests, also rightly, Da-sein's sense of being in a situation or context. We can join the two thoughts: Da-sein exists at every moment in some concrete context and does so understandingly. This understanding or "attunement" need not be reflective or thematic in any strong sense; its reality does not depend on intellection. Instead, contextual understanding underlies Da-sein's existence in the most pervasive way—and for this reason we often sense it only diffusely. "Mood" suggests a transient emotional cast "within" a person, but while this sort of phenomenon is certainly a foundational aspect of Da-sein's being (mood in this sense indicates clearly a "basic orientation," as defined above), Heidegger's intent is broader and subtler. Consider the following statement by Eugene Gendlin in *Focusing-Oriented Psychotherapy*:

> To experience something that is as yet unclear differs from experiencing an emotion; we know clearly that we are angry, or sad, or joyful. It also differs from familiar "feelings" even when these do not fall into universal categories. . . . What one senses at the "border zone" is unclear in that one does not know what to say or how to characterize it. Yet it is definite in that one senses unmistakably that it has its own unique quality. One cannot be talked out of this unique, unnamed quality, and one cannot be talked into feeling it as something else (1996, p. 17).

We see in operation his concept of felt sense: the experience of emergence. A person's experience of emergence, of situational process and unfolding, is not normally immediate in this sense. Gendlin says: "To stay with something directly felt requires a few seconds of silence" (p. 18). He then adds, like Heidegger: "It can be anxiety producing" (p. 18). Indeed, anxiety (in *Being and Time*) or uncanniness (in other writings) is the most telling type of experience in Da-sein's existence: It is the disclosing of being in the world as such, of the irremediable starkness of being t/here. Gendlin elaborates: "People are likely to go on talking, and to move to something else, and soon again to a still further point. In that way people mostly stay outside of themselves" (p. 18). Again, Heidegger makes much the same points in *Being and Time* and elsewhere, as we will see later.

Gendlin summarizes the characteristics of a felt sense thus:

> 1. A felt sense forms at the border zone between conscious and unconscious.
> 2. The felt sense has at first only an unclear quality (although unique and unmistakable).
> 3. The felt sense is experienced bodily.
> 4. The felt sense is experienced as a whole, a single datum that is internally complex.
> 5. The felt sense moves through steps; it shifts and opens step by step.
> 6. A step brings one closer to being that self which is not any content.
> 7. The process step has its own growth direction.
> 8. Theoretical explanations of a step can be devised only retrospectively (p. 24).

Gendlin's points 1 and 2 remind us of Heidegger's attention to emergence, construed generally; points 3 and 4 echo his respect for context and the whole; points 5, 6, and 7 sound again his preoccupation with process. Point 8 expresses the same therapeutic protocol that Boss articulates: "the whole of daseinsanalysis, what Heidegger's teaching has taught me" is "only to open my eyes":

> And also this is the whole direction that phenomenology or daseinsanalysis can give to a patient: to help him to open his eyes and to look at the things themselves and not to build theories beforehand and then to look through the theories to the human being (1988, p. 41).

Befindlichkeit means, "how Da-sein finds itself." The question in everyday language would be, "How are you?", to take up one of Gendlin's suggestions in "Befindlichkeit: Heidegger and the Philosophy of Psychology" (1978–1979, p. 45). We find ourselves . . . as we happen to find ourselves. We might find ourselves in one mood (in the narrow sense) or another, or in some context or other, or engaged in this path or that, but we always find ourselves . . . somehow. "We always find ourselves, somehow"—Da-sein always and already lives out a pre-understanding of itself, others, and world. Hermeneutic or interpretive understanding is necessarily circular, and this is a virtuous, not vicious, circle, in Heidegger's view. Kockelmans says:

> [T]he issues raised against Husserl's phenomenology imply that phenomenology can never present us with a presuppositionless philosophy.

But if this is so then what is needed is not a transcendental phenomenology in the sense of Husserl, but rather a hermeneutic phenomenology in the sense of Heidegger (1995, p. 535).

Heideggerian hermeneutic phenomenology, then, enjoins us to begin . . . where we already are. Phenomenology means, Heidegger stipulates, "*specifically engaging in our relationship to what we encounter* in which we always sojourn. In a sense, what is characteristic of phenomenology is the act of will not to resist this engaging-oneself", which is not, however, "a mere making myself conscious of my mode of being", which is a non-originative sort of awareness or experience (2001, p. 110). Our answer to the question, "How are you?", might prove vague, as we often find ourselves unable, at least immediately, to establish content, yet this stock question points to the ubiquity of finding ourselves. Finding ourselves is a root of our receiving-perceiving. Heidegger says in the *Seminars*: "In each case the *Who* exhausts itself precisely in the comportments in which I am [it is] involved just now" (p. 159). Receiving-perceiving implies awareness and understanding of our being t/here—our enworlded reality as human beings. Gendlin continues:

> [W]e saw how the concept {{of *Befindlichkeit*}} precedes and eliminates the distinction between *inside and outside*, as well as between *self and others*. Similarly, it alters *affective/cognitive*. Later I will also show how it also alters the distinctions we are used to in space and time: here/there, and past/present/future. . . . [S]uch basic changes in the kind of concept must affect any science, not just psychology (1978–1979, p. 47).

In sum, psychology should heed the "who" of Da-sein, Da-sein's self-understanding as a texture of openness in the broadest sense.

Boss uses the question "Why not?" as a psychotherapeutic strategy. We hear the echo of Heidegger's question in *An Introduction to Metaphysics*, "Why is there something rather than nothing?". His intent is to set into relief the client's being in the world as such. While the client always and already has an understanding of being in the world, this understanding is compromised constantly by the pull of irresoluteness. Forgetting the decisiveness of being in the world is a basic feature of being in the world. "Why not?" provokes Da-sein to recollect its truth as an active being in the midst of circumstances that nevertheless surpass the provenance of its action. As Heidegger elaborates:

> Possibilities, the possibilities of Dasein, are not a subject's tendencies or capacities. They always result, so to say, only from "outside," that is, from the particular historical situation of being-able-to-comport-oneself and of choosing, from the comportment toward what is encountered (2001, p. 158).

The inscrutability of contingency turns Da-sein back to its own felt essence as receiving-perceiving, as a processive being who is an opening t/here. The "finding" of anxiety, its revelatory power, Heidegger says, attests to our primal stand as beings in a world. The uncanniness of anxiety, as extraordinary as it is, is not a supernatural or otherworldly strangeness but the recurrently recovered recognition of the starkness of our basic condition. Heidegger says in *Being and Time*:

> Being-anxious discloses, primordially and directly, the world as world. It is not the case, say, that the world first gets thought of by deliberating about it, just by itself, . . . and that, in the face of this world anxiety then arises; what is rather the case is that the *world as world* is disclosed first and foremost by anxiety, as a mode of state-of-mind (1962, p. 232).

Fear concerns a specific object within the world; anxiety concerns the pressing reality of the world as such. Da-sein experiences in anxiety a more vital understanding of its own t/hereness and pro-jective activity; it experiences the "stress of address." This hermeneutic revelation, while salutary in principle, may startle Da-sein into retreat, yet even this obfuscatory mollification is a way in which Da-sein feels and senses, cognizes, thinks, ponders, chooses, and acts. We might call this phenomenon rationalization, to use ordinary parlance. A rationalization is an attempt to plaster over a rough truth, mitigating its force—and stretching for an alternative reading that lends a respectable or pleasing air. It is, in Freudian terms, a prevaricating maneuver of sham validation that muddies the reality of an inadmissible fact or condition of the grasping unconscious. Da-sein's preferred complacency is, in the first instance, a reaction to its own being, rather than just some piece of its psychology, which is a smaller category. Da-sein's ownmost possibilities include the possibility of disowning, or dissociation. We should heed Nietzsche's warning in *Twilight of the Idols* against a consoling but unrealistic belief in a "permanent daylight—the daylight of reason" (1982b, p. 478). The soberness of the insight that anxiety affords Da-sein bears the character of nothingness, or nowhereness: Anxiety is indefinite because it implicates everything and thus nothing (in particular). This quality is a no-thing-ness, but it is not merely nothing. Anxiety discloses world.

Heidegger entertains in the *Seminars* the naturalistic sounding concept of organismic stress, but he interprets and uses it phenomenologically and existentially. He admits that "[t]his reduction of being-in-the-world to the intensity of a stimulus [as in touching a hot plate] does exist and, for instance, plays a great role in pain" (2001, p. 209). Heidegger emphasizes, however, in keeping with his fundamental orientation, that "this being burdened {{by the impingement of other beings}}—the stress—belongs to the essential constitution of the *existing human being*" (p. 137; emphasis added). He continues: "As long as we think of the human being as a world-less Ego, the necessity of stress for life cannot be made intelligible" (p. 137). Stress is the reality of being addressed: "Stress means a *claim on one*" (p. 141). Things address Da-sein as a receiving-perceiving openness, and Da-sein responds . . . in this way or that way. The pressure of world is not incidental or deflectable—it defines Da-sein's basic position as being t/here. Heidegger reviews his speculations thus:

> [S]tress belongs to the essential connection of address and response, that is to the dimension of conversation in the broad sense, including a "speaking" with things as well. Once again, conversation forms the fundamental domain within which an interpretation becomes possible. Thus, the "hermeneutic circle" is not a *circulus vitiosus*, but an essential constitution of human being. It characterizes the finitude of the human being. The human being, in his highest being, is limited precisely by his openness to being (p. 140).

Da-sein's openness to being, its being an opening, presupposes closing and the opaque truth of the closed. Da-sein's existence as a bounded being, as a mortal, establishes the tone of its conversation with things and its end as an opening through which being is articulated. The stress of address is not essentially a causal phenomenon; it is a matter of what Heidegger calls motive (an issue to which we will turn later): "*Motive*: 'Movement'—what addresses me [but] does not cause [something in me]" (p. 209).

Heidegger also treats a mood or "finding" that we might view initially as the antipode of anxiety: boredom. For him, though, boredom reveals almost as much about Da-sein's enworlded character as anxiety. Heidegger distinguishes the two thus: "In boredom a removal [*Sich-entziehen*] of beings as a whole occurs, but [it is] not a total slipping away [*Verschwinden*] [of beings], as in anxiety" (p. 209). Anxiety is a "total slipping away" of individual things, leaving Da-sein with an intensely felt sense of being enworlded as such. Boredom is a "removal of beings as a whole," thus again leaving a sense of being enworlded as such—but individual things remain, as empty and unsatisfying. No sense of being overwhelmed oppresses Da-sein in boredom; the problem is a perceived lack of meaning or worth. Nothing fulfills. Boredom is one of the principal diseases of the postmodern world, so his thoughts on the matter are still perfectly relevant. Heidegger discusses boredom at length in *The Fundamental Concepts of Metaphysics: World, Finitude, Solitude*, making it a central feature of his thinking immediately after the publication of *Being and Time*. He wonders whether his cultural age (circa 1929), which appears indifferent, is asleep: "Is this questionable profound boredom actually supposed to be the *sought-after fundamental attunement* that must be *awakened*? (1995, p. 77). Heidegger demarcates three "forms of boredom": (i) "becoming bored by something," (ii) "being bored with something and the kind of passing the time pertaining to it," and (iii) "profound boredom as 'it is boring for one'" (pp. ix–xi). He warns his readers against employing only a psychological—a merely regional or localized—reading of this phenomenon: "We must do this {{investigate boredom}}, . . . not in the sense of dissecting some psychological experience, but in such a way that we thereby approach ourselves. Whom? Ourselves—*ourselves as a Da-sein*" (p. 82).

The first form of boredom demonstrates an obvious feature: being bored by . . . x. Some thing bores us (for example, "This book is becoming tedious"). This form involves "passing the time so that we *do not need to listen to it*" (p. 136). The second form adds another obvious and crucial feature: We are bored by . . . x . . . in a temporal way. Time "stretches" or "empties" in boredom (for example, "This presentation is going on forever"). This form involves "*not wanting to listen*" (p. 136). Heidegger's analysis of the third form of boredom includes the first two forms but deepens the interpretation by focusing on the identity of the one who experiences boredom, Da-sein. This form, unlike the first two, involves "*being compelled to listen*, . . . in the sense of that kind of compelling force which everything *properly authentic* about Dasein possesses, and which accordingly is related to Dasein's *innermost freedom*" (p. 136). Heidegger explains that the indifference of boredom is a broad and complex feeling (or Gestalt), not merely a "sum total of evaluations" (p. 138). Boredom in its deepest significance discloses the profundity of Da-sein's being in the world as such. Beings as a whole show an indifference that is a "telling refusal," which is a "making manifest" of how Da-sein stands (p. 138, p. 139). The withdrawal of beings in boredom is global yet ambiguous: "The emptiness is not a hole between things that are filled, but concerns beings as a whole and yet is *not* the *Nothing*" (p. 140). Heidegger reminds us that boredom, though it may seem to be the stoppage of time, must be an event in or of time, so boredom must be interpreted "in terms of originary temporality" (p. 141). The boring spans beings as a whole backwardly and forwardly; Da-sein is unable to gain purchase; a locus is lacking. Da-sein is clasped by emptiness that spans beings, and this is "the originary manner in which the attunement that we call boredom attunes us" (p. 144).

Heidegger speaks of a "moment of vision" in which Da-sein is disclosed to itself in boredom (p. 149):

> [T]his peculiar impoverishment which sets in with respect to ourselves in this "it is boring for one" first *brings* the *self* in all its nakedness *to itself* as the self that *is there* and has taken over the being-there of its Da-sein. For what purpose? *To be that Da-sein*. Beings as a whole refuse themselves tellingly, not to me as me, but to the Dasein in me whenever I know that "it is boring for one" (p. 143).

This moment of vision is ambiguous inasmuch as it is "announced in this telling refusal"—an experience of withdrawal or "need" is a condition of insight (p. 169, p. 162). Boredom can instruct, but only if we allow ourselves to suffer the discomfort of tarrying with it. We should heed *"profound boredom"* (p. 159). Heidegger's thinking contains no facile positive truths or enunciations. The "one" who experiences boredom is the human being as Da-sein, and since Da-sein is temporal, being and time coalesce powerfully in the event of boredom that offers a moment of vision. Indeed, as he claims in *The Concept of Time*: "Dasein, conceived in its most extreme possibility of Being, *is time itself*, not *in* time" (1992, 13E-14E). Being t/here as time experiences in boredom the sway and vicissitudes of its temporalizing. Heidegger asserts: "It is not beings that properly refuse, but time, which itself makes possible the manifestness of these beings as a whole" (1995, p. 150). Beings themselves do not withdraw—beings *as things of concern* to being t/here *as time* lose their typical lure. Da-sein is concerned with things in time, not with any sort of Kantian thing-in-itself beyond time; boredom is a phenomenon of the human being as enworlded and concernful being t/here. Heidegger highlights repeatedly the defining reality of Da-sein's temporalizing in explaining boredom, rather than following the superficial clue of the qualities of things that bore. He makes the following remarkable statement:

> Because things and people are enveloped by temporality and permeated by it, even though it is temporality in itself which properly and singularly bores us, the legitimate illusion can arise that things are boring, and that it is people themselves who are bored (p. 158).

The origin of boredom is temporality itself: *"temporality as such"* is what bores (p. 158). Being /there as time is boring. If Da-sein ponders well the experience of profound boredom and thus its own basic condition, it may find the freedom "to be that Da-sein" as time.

3. Time and Temporality

Heidegger's heavy emphasis on time and temporality is one respect in which his thinking bears upon psychotherapy in an especially distinctive way. To use an obvious (and perhaps the most apposite) example, Freud's approach is founded upon a strong conception of human beings as historical. A person's present character and behaviors are intelligible only by deep reference to the person's past experiences such that only a specialized analytic archeology can reveal the truth of psyche. Furthermore, only a trained analyst can be in a position to establish this intelligibility. Heidegger's direction is less specialized and perhaps more intuitive, although no less exacting. He takes up the issue of time, temporality, and historicity in such a way that we, as dwelling mortals, can take up this issue for ourselves. The word archeology shows the difference between Freud's psychoanalytic approach and Heidegger's hermeneutic-phenomenological orientation. The first presupposes an "under-realm," a paranoumenal reality that does not allow direct admittance, while the second presupposes access and understanding, and investigates what appears as it appears.

In fairness, however, we must admit frankly that Heidegger's thinking cannot be described accurately as Apollonian; he does not believe that the nature of things is usually plain. He maintains throughout his career in different ways that our reality, the reality of being, is ambiguous. Heidegger considers concealment, and indeed the concealment of concealment, to be as primordial as unconcealment. (Recall Nietzsche's dismissal of the impossible—or simply unhealthy—ideal of a "permanent daylight of reason.") Even so, this ambiguity is of a different sort from Freud's bifurcated (or trifurcated) psychological reality. Heideggerian concealment is itself a phenomenon within our experience (in need of attention and appropriation, naturally), whereas (traditional) depth psychology's emphasis on the unconscious, on some views, implies a radical split within the human being—two worlds. Boss, as a notable example, attempted to retain psychoanalytic practices while avoiding this pitfall. Granted, all psychotherapeutic approaches (not just psychoanalysis) must assume and employ some sense of history, since all clients or patients exist temporally and bear histories. We could say that Heidegger's meditation upon *die Sache selbst* (the matter of thinking itself) exposes temporality's mystery as utterly originative in human life, that this phenomenon of mystery is nevertheless a living reality for us, and that this interpretation does not contradict our earlier point about access and understanding. We exist in time, or, as he says more strongly in *The Concept of Time*, we *are* time, in which case we have both access to and understanding of time, an understanding that involves an acknowledgment of our temporality's "ecstatic" character. We can write ecstatic as ek-static to emphasize the aspect of "standing (or stepping) outside" that distinguishes the human type of being. Heidegger says in *The Concept of Time*: "In running ahead Dasein *is* its future, in such a way that in this being futural it comes back to its own past and present. Dasein, conceived in its most extreme possibility of Being, *is time itself*, not *in* time" (1992, pp. 13E–14E). He characterizes Da-sein's very appearance in the world as *Geworfenheit* or "thrownness": We are thrown into our world. Furthermore, Da-sein chooses or "throws forward" this possibility, this way of being in the world, but not others. It chooses not only the meaning of its past and present, but most vitally its future. Hence, Da-sein is never a settled being, but a movement and a question. (Compare Nietzsche on this account, despite the obvious differences between the orientations of the two thinkers.) Holmes says: "Because Dasein temporalizes itself, which is to say comes towards itself from the future in accordance with the projects for-the-sake-of-which it is now engaged, it makes possible a 'there'—a 'here' where Dasein is not" (1995, p. 40). Lived time, not measured or technical time, Heidegger avers in the *Seminars*, is the manner in which being-in-the-world dwells in the first instance:

> Saying "today," "yesterday," and "tomorrow" is, ... a more original comportment toward time than ascertaining "how much" time by the clock. Ascertaining time by the clock is merely a calculative determination of the particular today, yesterday, and tomorrow. We can always use a clock because there is a today, a tomorrow, and a yesterday for us in advance, ... (2001, p. 41).

Technical time shows us only "the now, but no clock ever shows the future or has ever shown the past" (1992, p. 17E). As a kinetic opening, Da-sein is time-ly: "[T]here is obviously something necessary about the belonging together of time and the human being's unfolding essence" (2001, p. 38). Heidegger insists on the ek-static coalescence of time and the human being's unfolding essence as the most primal phenomenon of Da-sein as time: "In terms of priority, this belonging together is the first and not, as it might appear, the third element which results from putting the human being and time together" (p. 38). As being-in-the-world, Da-sein becomes what it is through its gathering movement into the future, a process that ends only with death, which "reveals itself as that *possibility which is one's ownmost, which is non-relational, and which is not to be outstripped*" (1962, p. 294). Short of the end of being-in-the-world, Da-sein as an opening not only "has" a history but is historicity itself (1992, p. 20E).

Psychotherapy explores the client's "unfolding essence," and thus the client's time-ly dwelling as being-in-the-world. Some psychotherapeutic approaches focus heavily on past events, while some pay little attention to a client's past and instead stress the present as the gateway to the future. In these days of short-term psychotherapy, some praxes emphasize "managing" the present for the sake of a more "effective" future. A better future is certainly a desirable state of affairs, and Heidegger's rationale for offering the seminars in Zollikon is indeed the amelioration of problems in living. On his view, though, Da-sein ek-sists simultaneously in past, present, and future. The original present is never just a "now" or dot on a merely quantitative and therefore indifferent continuum of dots. The present is our being-in-the-world as care-ful, engaged activity. Time is always and already *my* time; a lived world of purely impersonal and thus hollow temporal instants would be a surd (and a typical symptom of clinical depression). Furthermore, Da-sein's present activity aims toward .... It is futural. The now extends into the not-yet. Da-sein is always and already "underway." Finally, the now and the not-yet are informed by the past or already-been. So no temporal dimension is dead, passive, or unconnected. Heidegger says in *The Concept of Time*:

For the most part, Dasein is there in everydayness. Everydayness, however, as that particular temporality which flees in the face of futuricity, can only be understood when confronted with the authentic time of the futural being of the past (p. 19E).

Such a statement would be unintelligible in the absence of his ek-static conception of time. First, Da-sein in its everydayness "flees in the face of futuricity": It shrinks at the prospect of a chosen future for which it is responsible in the deepest way. This point is simple. Second, what is the "futural being of the past?" Heidegger speaks of death as *"Dasein's running ahead to its past, to an extreme possibility of itself that stands before it in certainty and utter indeterminacy"* (p. 12E). "Running ahead to the past" is possible because Da-sein is a being-in-the-world who knows that no-longer-being-in-the-world is inevitable. Death will overtake Da-sein eventually (it is "not to be outstripped"), and Da-sein knows this truth of its condition. Heidegger calls death a possibility because Da-sein must appropriate it in one way or another; it is a factical reality of being-in-the-world, but not a mere fact like others in the world. Death is one of an individual's ownmost prospects, not a matter of nonchalence or abstraction. Since death is an inevitable factical reality that Da-sein must interpret in this way or that way, we can, without inconsistency, say that death is a certainty (death will happen), a possibility (Da-sein must decide upon the meaning of this factical certainty), and an indeterminacy (no ready-made meaning suffices, for the individual must die his or her *own* death, usually at an unknown time). The "futural being of the past" is death's effect on our understanding of where we have been: Our past is an interpretive ingredient in our present contemplation of future death. We cannot literally run ahead to the past, but we must do so interpretively as beings who dwell ek-statically in yesterday, today, and tomorrow. Heidegger says: "For the most part I know of death in the manner of a knowing that shrinks back" (p. 12E). This shrinking back is part of everyday Da-sein as time, not an incidental variation or result. Da-sein also shrinks away from its past. A distracting present is the remedy for the demands of appropriating conscientiously one's ek-sistence as a whole: "Dasein as clinging to its present says: the past is what is past, irretrievable. This is the past of the everyday present which resides in the present of its busyness. This is why Dasein, thus determined as present, fails to see what is past" (p. 19E). Da-sein "loses itself in its material" (p. 19E). Whether "authentic" or "inauthentic" (terms that we will later treat at greater length), Da-sein's sojourning as a time-ly being is a structurally integrated process in which all three temporal dimensions live simultaneously, with the future, on Heidegger's view, as the distinctive facet for being-in-the-world as throwing thrownness. Da-sein's being underway is a running ahead: "*[T]he fundamental phenomenon of time is the future*" (p. 14E). He opines in "Time and Being":

To talk of what is coming toward us has meanwhile become a cliché. Thus we hear: "the future has already begun," which is not so, because the future never just begins since absence, as the presencing of what is not yet present, always in some way already concerns us, is present no less immediately than what has been (1972, p. 13).

As Heidegger says simply in the *Seminars*: "*Everything begins with the future!*" (2001, p. 159).

As care, Da-sein is underway in its world of engagements and pro-jects. Its most important temporal dimension is futurity, as being-in-the-world is always moving along to . . . . This holds true even when "not much is happening," or, as we have seen, in boredom. Un/concealing happens at every point of Da-sein's ek-sistence—else Da-sein would not be being t/here—even when Da-sein finds the vibrancy of its futurity waning. An ek-sistence with little or unreliable futural vibrancy is a compromised sojourning. As it is, Da-sein in its everyday manner of being in the world is futural yet flees in the face of futurity and is historical yet fails to see what is past. Clinical issues that involve compromised futurity thus compound and distort Da-sein's already ambiguous being-as-time and aggravate any infelicities that result from such. Da-sein as a kinetic opening is free, a freedom for . . . . As clinically troubled being-in-the-world, Da-sein's openness dwindles to the point of felt incapacity. Being-in-the-world's futural freedom for . . . becomes a constricted movement, a narrowed engagement of world as care-ful reality. At the same time, this attenuation of the openness of being in the world makes itself felt to Da-sein as a call to what is ownmost. Da-sein's most intimate possibilities as an individual mortal unfolding in openness begin to recede, thereby reminding Da-sein of their abiding force. Heidegger says in the *Seminars*:

> Stress means a *claim on one* [*Beanspruchung*], and that [claim] initially in an excessive manner. In general, a claim on one requires some kind of response at any given time to which privations also belong, such as the fact of not responding and of not being able to respond (p. 141).

When Da-sein finds itself unable to respond satisfactorily to "what addresses Da-sein from the openness of its world," it suffers from "disturbances in adjustment and freedom":

> We do psychology, sociology, and psychotherapy in order to help the human being reach the goal of adjustment and freedom in the broadest sense. This is the joint concern of physicians and sociologists because all social and pathological disturbances of the individual human being are disturbances in adjustment and freedom (p. 151, p. 154).

The amelioration of disturbances in adjustment and freedom is a time-ly endeavor: The therapist or counselor must help the individual by calling him back to his character as ek-static being-in-the-world who chooses presently the meaning of past and future—his sense of sojourning as such. The past is not definitive, as it is under a psychoanalytic regime. Instead, the client feels a constriction of movement toward . . . . A feeling of being mired in an unsatisfying present presupposes being-toward-the-future. Even preoccupations with the past are futural concerns inasmuch as Da-sein understands its past for the sake of understanding pro-jectively its future. Running ahead to the future is a going back to the past that takes up the present in an organic movement of projective determination of meaning. In other words: Da-sein is a care-ful ek-static being (in/as time). Heidegger says:

> The human being's richness consists precisely [in the fact] that he is not dependent upon the mere presence of a sequence of "nows," through which I cannot understand the whole of being and whereby it remains closed [to me] that Da-sein, in its unfolding essence, has emerged into the fullness of these [temporal] modalities (pp. 179–180).

The intertwined fullness of these temporal modalities holds sway despite the seeming existence of contrary examples:

> That little children and old people live exclusively in the present does not mean that the two cases are the same. On the contrary, one must not cut off the ecstatic [dimension]. In contrast to the small child, the old person has having-been-ness [*Gewesen-sein*], but it conceals itself (p. 183).

A small child is on the way to being a mature Da-sein; it is not yet a fully formed instance of being-in-the-world. Its past is minute and not usually an explicitly pressing matter of concern. Its sense of the future is real enough but still primitive. The old person dwells in a world in which history is long and the future, as the determination of the meaning of the past as it is taken up in life's final movements, is more imperative than ever. In Heidegger's view, the old person's character of living in the present is not simple but a more closely integrated felt complex of the three temporal modalities in light of the inevitability of ownmostness. Boss says:

> In discussing these extreme illnesses, we have studiously avoided claiming that the temporal extensions are ever actually lost, saying rather that they are masked, or covered up. . . . Being essential to human nature, none of them can simply disappear and still leave a human *Da-sein* behind (1994, p. 214).

Da-sein: Opening Thoughts 31

If Da-sein *is* time, as Heidegger asserts, and if time is past, present, and future, then Da-sein must always and already be all three of the temporal ek-stases of its being-in-the-world. In any event, we must return shortly to the complex question of hiddenness.

Two

DA-SEIN: INTEGRAL REALITIES

1. Consciousness

Heidegger, unlike Descartes and many who have followed, avoids appealing to "consciousness" or the like as the effective or ultimate center of our being. Indeed, as he notes, the term consciousness "has been in use only since the eighteenth century," at which time it "acquired the theoretical meaning of the relationship to objects, which can be experienced {{by the self-conscious self}}" (2001, p. 225, p. 226). (Heidegger mentions explicitly Descartes, whose philosophy comprises in great measure a complementary response to the rise of modern Western science.) The notion of consciousness privileges the singular quality of transparency in perceiving what is present, but without inquiring into the full character of this lucidity and what grants it in the first place. It also does not see the danger of the possibility of shifting unwittingly from a kind of clarity to a fixing and controlling stare—in other words, the problem of egotism. We should, as surprising as it may seem, leave behind "cognition" as well, since it assumes, as Heidegger sees the matter, a more or less motorized view of the human being that smacks of scientism. The notion of cognition emphasizes the mechanics and technicalities of Da-sein's receiving-perceiving at the expense of a wider and more penetrating account of the ways in which Da-sein exists in the world with other human beings and physical things. Cognitively oriented approaches, in their strong forms, can render the human being either a cyborg or a mere animal. We must be clear: Heidegger does not, and cannot coherently, deny the reality or importance of our physical being, including our sensory, perceptual, and higher order neurological systems and processes. His aim, however, is a faithful interpretation of Da-sein's existence in its essential fullness, not just the mechanical or technical aspects. Consciousness and cognition, in other words, imply perspectives on the human being that Heidegger considers as unthought originally—indeed, in the final analysis, as baneful. Being t/here makes intelligible consciousness and cognition, whereas consciousness and cognition, even construed generously, cannot account for the elemental fact or truth of Da-sein as being t/here.

If Heidegger eschews the notion of consciousness, how does he account for our awareness? The answer is surprisingly simple. The German word for consciousness is *Bewissen*; according to Heidegger: "This means that someone finds his way" (p. 225).

The question is whether this "finding one's way" amidst things present-at-hand, whether this consciousness is the presupposition for Da-sein, or whether Da-sein, that is the sojourning in the open {{Da}}, provides the possibility for comportment in the first place, in the sense of "finding one's way," thus, of consciousness. Obviously, the second is the case. (pp. 225–226).

The notion of consciousness is intelligible enough, but we cannot grasp its tendentiousness and problematic digressiveness as long as we fail to see its status as a secondary phenomenon. As Heidegger says: "*Consciousness* always presupposes Da-sein, not conversely. Knowledge and consciousness are always already moving in the *openness of the Da*. Without this, they would not be possible at all" (p. 207). If we take what is derivative as primary, we misunderstand not only consciousness but also basic human awareness and the wholeness of our nature as human beings. We misread ourselves. Heidegger exhorts in *The Fundamental Concepts of Metaphysics*: "{{The point is}} *not to describe the consciousness of man but to evoke the Dasein in man*" (1995, p. 174).

2. The Unconscious

If the notion of consciousness does not suit Heidegger's approach to the question of being, then the notion of an unconscious is also unfitting. We might take his accent on concealment as comparable to the notion of an unconscious, but this would be a mistake. The two ideas involve distinct outlooks on the basic character of human existing as well as divergent practical remedies. The Heideggerian concept of concealment bears cosmological overtones; reality as a whole partakes in the kinesis of unconcealment, concealment, and the concealment of concealment. Da-sein can, through meditative questioning, come to appreciate better this human and trans-human reality. The full-bodied conception of an unconscious psyche, on the other hand, pertains only to human beings, and proper access to the unconscious psyche is available only through a set of specialized procedures that rest on a host of highly particular scientific, physical, and philosophical assumptions about human nature. Boss, Heidegger's chief associate in psychological research, states flatly: "It is . . . high time that the phrase psychic unconscious was expunged from the vocabulary of psychology and psychopathology" (1994, p. 141). He reasons:

Neither the clearing nor the hiddenness originates in concrete things, human beings, or in the psyche. Rather, this hiddenness is the mysterious source from which all that is comes forth to be. It is thus pretemporal, prespatial, and prehuman. And as it is also prelinguistic, the word itself {{hiddenness}} that designates this primal phenomenon represents only a makeshift solution fraught with the danger of being misleading (p. 142).

Heidegger's faith in language as the "saying" or working out of being may appear similar to the "talking cure" of classical psychoanalysis in which a patient articulates consciously, and thereby rights, the unevenness in her libidinal economy. The resemblance, however, is limited. The moment of explicit expression in Freud's consulting room is an episode of discharge, perhaps mechanical, not an articulation, in Heidegger's sense, of existential identity, decision, and meditative thinking about "the matter itself" by virtue of which we are as we are. Hermann Lang, Stefan Brunnhuber, and Rudolph F. Wagner argue in "The So-Called Zollikon Seminars—Heidegger as a Psychotherapist" that "[p]sychoanalysis is a 'hermeneutic' both in theory and practice" (2003, p. 353). They attribute at least some of Heidegger's criticisms of psychology to the influence of "Boss, the expert, {{who has}} given Heidegger, the psychotherapeutic and psychoanalytical layman, a picture of psychoanalysis that completely revolved around a mechanistic-technical world view" (p. 353). Lang, Brunnhuber, and Wagner argue further that "it is precisely psychoanalysis that meets the demands made by Heidegger" by emphasizing "the role of a listener" and how in both approaches the human being "is seen as a being intended for freedom" (p. 354). We will return to this question shortly.

Heidegger affirms the "who-ness" of Da-sein as being t/here: "When I forget something painful, I do not want to think about it. Here, *it* does not slip away from me, but *I* let it slip away from me" (2001, p. 169). Relation is a phenomenon of human existing in its fullness, which includes physicality, but relation even inasmuch as it involves physicality exceeds scientific measurement. For example, not letting something slip away means holding on to something, yet

> one cannot derive retaining from a container [the unconscious]. An "engram" {{unconscious deposit}} is never a retaining of something as something. An engram is a physiological change, but retaining is a relationship to something to which an understanding of being belongs. In contrast, an engram is a purely thinglike change. Retaining itself as such is not something physiological (p. 170).

Freud's system

> postulates {{regarding consciousness}} an unbroken [chain] of explanation, that is, the continuity of causal connections. Since there is no such thing "within consciousness," he has to invent "the unconscious" in which there must be an unbroken [chain of] causal connections.... This

postulate is not derived from the psychical phenomena themselves but is a *postulate* of modern natural science. (pp. 207–208).

We might well wonder why the inclusion of postulates in a system should be, in itself, such a cause for concern. Heidegger's slant on postulates, however, stresses their incomplete nature and therefore their philosophical thorniness. He distinguishes *acceptio* or acceptance and *suppositio* or supposition (and even notes that Aristotle deems as uneducated those who do not know this difference). We may understand acceptance in a particular case as phenomenological givenness or manifestation and supposition as proving something "by reducing it to a causal connection" (p. 187). Heidegger sees supposition that purports to be *acceptio*—science—as problematic, since, as he says in speaking of the body, "I cannot 'understand' something merely causal. That means that I can have no insight into how one thing is derived from something else, that is, how it originates *out from* it" (p. 186). This is a perplexing statement. What, then, is his sense of understanding?

> [The term] understanding may be used only regarding to {{sic}} an insight into the [contextual] connection between motives. Insight [describes] how something is connected with something else—when I can see the meaning of something someone is talking about and how something which was said corresponds to the matter intended (p. 186).

Understanding is rooted in the *Da* or open clearing in which we exist, that we are. It is a question of relation, process, interpretation, and existential appropriation within this allowance. Thus, to revisit Heidegger's example, remembering as an elemental event of Da-sein's dwelling is not essentially a set of causal determinants that lie beyond the non-scientist but a matter of direct human experience, decision, and import. Cohn points to "a more direct communication between therapist and client who share a world and are 'with each other' in what they meet. There is no need for the mediating scaffolding of 'representations' like 'projections' and 'transference'" (1999, p. 40). Science is effective but limited, Heidegger emphasizes: "The phenomenon of remembering cannot be grasped by the methods of natural science. Only the bodily-corporeal . . . conditions of its performance can be ascertained. These are two entirely different matters" (2001, p. 202). Cohn elaborates:

> [H]ermeneutic interpretation does not replace what is known with what is concealed, but any disclosure extends what is already known, and thus the total *understanding* of the total situation {{in contrast with "mere" explanation; emphasis added}}, though never fully reached, has been significantly increased (2002, p. 48).

Thus, for example, "[a]n unexpressed anger, . . . is an unexpressed anger, no more, no less. It is not an anger clamouring for expression and excluded from it. The fact that it is unexpressed is part of what it is" (pp. 61–62). Dealing with unexpressed anger means dealing with a present reality: interpreting and deciding about the anger, no matter how long standing, here and now. Da-sein cannot vivify a dead past, Cohn says, but it always responds interpretively—meaningfully and freely—to whatever it has brought along into its present. He contrasts psychoanalysis and existential therapy in the following way:

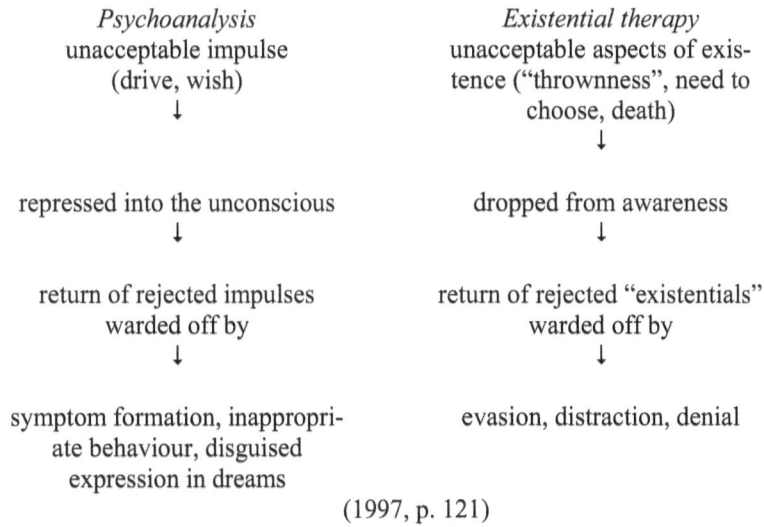

Psychoanalysis	*Existential therapy*
unacceptable impulse (drive, wish) ↓	unacceptable aspects of existence ("thrownness", need to choose, death) ↓
repressed into the unconscious ↓	dropped from awareness ↓
return of rejected impulses warded off by ↓	return of rejected "existentials" warded off by ↓
symptom formation, inappropriate behaviour, disguised expression in dreams	evasion, distraction, denial

(1997, p. 121)

William J. Richardson distinguishes in "Truth and Freedom in Psychoanalysis" Heidegger's concepts of "rendering something present"—bringing it near not physically but intentionally, in "the mind's eye"—and "recalling" it—retrieving a "content"—explaining that the former "will enable him {{Heidegger}} to explain certain parapraxes (like forgetting one's umbrella) without resorting to the notion of some unconscious wish" (2003, p. 80).

The question of the relationship between the thinking of Heidegger and Freud is basic, at least because Boss educated Heidegger about Freudian psychology and Heidegger spends a fair amount of time the *Seminars* on matters of Freudian and scientific psychology. Fred Dallmayr takes up this question in "Heidegger and Freud." He indicates at the outset that Heidegger's way of understanding the human being makes room for the "quality of human phenomena," in contrast with the Freudian orientation toward (quantitative) forces (1995, p. 550). Heidegger premises his outlook on Da-sein as a "care-ful" or concerned and involved being for whom the "urgency" of drives is just one instance of its general heedfulness or beholdenness to itself, others, and things

(p. 550). Being t/here means that Da-sein is claimed or addressed by its world, by its being; the concept of force is a particular interpretation that lies within the pale of Da-sein's responsiveness to the claim or address of world. Specialized concepts of force such as introjection, projection, and transference devolve from the primal reality of Da-sein's being-with others, but are quantifying, mechanistic derivatives of this fundamental "co-being" (p. 551). The being-in-the-world of the one "blends" with the being-in-the-world of the other (p. 551). Forces are not shunted across a gap from this container to that capsule over there. "The ego," says Dallmayr, "was only a narrow crystallization of being-in-the-world, valid for limited purposes and in restricted contexts" (p. 551).

We find in Heidegger an acknowledgment of a clearing that both reveals and conceals, but the concealing aspect of this clearing is not tantamount to the occlusive pit of the unconscious. Under Freud's scheme, repressed "stuff" resides restlessly in a densely involuted psychic bog. According to Heidegger's story, the clearing in which Da-sein dwells is un/covering: a simultaneous presenting and withdrawing. Sheehan, in "On Movement and the Destruction of Ontology", speaks of "pres-ab-sential bivalence": the two-fold processive truth of openness as the kinetics of the cosmos (1981, p. 540). As Heidegger claims in "On the Essence of Truth," untruth or concealment is co-extensive with truth as unconcealment. Layers and degrees of un/concealing comprise Da-sein's "ontological exposure" as receiving/perceiving, but concealment is not an under-realm or an inner compartment, as Heidegger takes pains to show in the *Seminars* (2001, p. 560). Da-sein's exposure as openness renders it liable to lethic influence—the sway of forgetting—yet this sway is integral to the freedom of being receiving-perceiving. Even so, we could attempt to make connections between Heidegger's thinking and neo-Freudian theories, such that the distance between Heidegger and psychology inspired by Freud diminishes and stronger affinities emerge. Dallmayr, in discussing the compatibilist Richardson and the incompatibilist Kockelmans, relates Richardson's affirmation of Da-sein as an ek-static and therefore de-centered ("ex-centric") self (1995, p. 559). Dallmayr's point is that extending this gloss brings the Heideggerian self closer to, among other points of reference, the Lacanian self. We will return to the question of a de-centered self, though not in an effort to connect Heidegger with later, more "postmodern" ways of thinking. For the moment, we will note that Thompson asserts:

> With no leg to stand on, even its own, postmodernism as it is currently envisioned appears to define itself as a paradigm of spiritual emptiness, a cul-de-sac that is impervious to either passion or purpose. Having abandoned any vestige of selfhood or history, it depicts a world that is, perhaps contentedly, finally alienated from its own alienation (2004, p. 198).

He claims that postmodernism lacks "a heart"—but that Heideggerian thinking has one (p. 198).

Mills explores the relation between Hegel and Freud in *The Unconscious Abyss: Hegel's Anticipation of Psychoanalysis*. He admits that Hegel makes few explicit references to the unconscious, but believes that a perspective on the unconscious which is fundamental to Hegel's thinking emerges upon careful textual inspection. Mills's treatment is pertinent because he shows the affinities between the Hegelian and Freudian rudiments of process, emergence, and opacity—or, in Heideggerian terms, un/concealing. Heidegger accentuates beings as beings: persons and things as ontological coalescences and movements that appear and show themselves but always with a measure of reticence. (In Gestalt terms, a perceiver cannot experience all perspectives at the same time. Perspective is contextual and reflexive.) As with Hegel's abyss and Freud's unconscious, this reticence originates beyond the power of individual persons and things. Being is inherently, and not incidentally, mysterious. Heidegger is not a monger of obfuscation or ambage, but a witness to the ineluctable reality of ineffability and withdrawal. His ruminations about occlusion resemble, at least roughly, the intimation of Mills's Hegel that our primal identity as beings includes a living yet reluctant source, a "difference" that is central to identity. Heidegger's statements about historical unfolding (for example, in "The Question Concerning Technology") prod us to admit the ever-present and powerful reality of kinetics beyond immediate awareness and control, an idea to which Freud would assent in general terms. Mills sees both Hegel and Freud as embracing the outlook that the world is a "dynamic flux of transposing and self-generative, creative processes having their form and instantiability within the dialectic of becoming" (2002, p. 194). Heidegger shares this appreciation of process and the sway of energies that inform the history of human beings in general and the histories of individual Da-seins. Does, he, though, come appreciably close to a psychoanalytic notion of the unconscious? Heidegger's own words suggest that a correspondence of this sort is not possible. He insists on the who-ness of Da-sein, and the clearing of the *Da*, even with its shadowy edges and trans-human hinterland, is not Freud's "seething cauldron of excitation" or even, less dramatically, a psychoanalytic system of indications for which the ideal of translation is the most apt ingress. Both Heidegger (for instance, his "being compelled to listen" to boredom) and Freud (with his patients in his consulting room) emphasize listening: to what being says, for Heidegger, and to the serpentine articulations of the id, for Freud. Again, Lang, Brunnhuber, and Wagner highlight "the role of a listener" in Freud's praxis in arguing that his approach satisfies Heidegger's challenges in the *Seminars*. They call for practicing "the art of asking questions" with the aim of "the other person becoming free so that he can take responsibility for his own life" (2003, p. 355). Richardson states that "[t]he whole process of psychoanalysis is reducible, . . . to the talking of a subject to an analyst who listens—hence the etiquette 'talking cure'" (2003, p. 86). This prescription as stated is consistent with (as we will see) Heidegger's support for "anticipatory care" that encourages the client to live a freer and more responsible existence instead of "intervening care" that steps in for the client and thus leaves him comparatively dependent and inarticulate. Even so, both mainstream Freudian theory and practice differ considerably from Heidegger's philosophical orientation, and they may be incommensurable. This is an intricate question, as affinities exist—but affinities exist across any number of perspectives. The best hope for compatibility may be Mills's synthetic "process psychology," which shows uncommonly adroit attentiveness to the broad elements that span the stances of Heidegger, Freud, and Hegel: process, un/concealing, articulation, freedom.

3. Action

We have seen Heidegger's emphasis on Da-sein's openness and freedom, but have hardly exhausted his conception of freedom. Da-sein acts in freedom, but how? Freedom implies moving toward or away from something, but this structure might suggest a causal interpretation. After all, moving toward and away sound like attraction and aversion in psychology and biology, or attraction and repulsion in Hobbes's mechanistic universe of dynamic atoms. Can we account for motive by way of psychology, biology, or physics, with little or no reference to a robust conception of freedom? Heidegger thinks not. Freedom and motive, in his view, are distinct yet ever-paired aspects of Da-sein's existing in the world. The following exchange from the *Seminars* highlights this truth of existence:

> SP {{seminar participant}}: No, it's not a necessary sequence {{"closing the window *because* it's noisy outside"; emphasis added}}. There's freedom in it.
> MH: Where's the freedom?
> SP: It can be a decision between two motives, for example, pleasure and lack of pleasure. We follow the stronger stimulus.
> MH: What is motive now? That which determines {{"determines"}} me to close the window. Motive calls forth free will. It does not restrict it. Motive is not coercive. One is unconstrained—free. Motive addresses me for something.... (2001, pp. 21–22)

Heidegger asserts: "Noise is not the cause of getting up" (p. 22). He asks:

> What kind of ground is a motive? The familiar world is needed for that—the context of the world in which I live. A cause follows according to a rule. In contrast, nothing like this is required for determining a motive.

The motive's characteristic is that it moves me and that it addresses the human being. There is obviously something in a motive that addresses me. There is an understanding, a being open for a specific context of significance in the world (p. 23).

Heidegger goes on to call causality "the ground for sequences within the process of nature" and motive "a ground for human action"—and hastens to add: "All that is has a ground" (p. 23). Ground in its essence is unthought in science, he believes.

Heidegger admits the reality of what he identifies as motive but refuses a causal construal. Understanding the world by way of causation requires considering human actions as "sequences" within an epistemically tractable and regularized physical nature. Da-sein's actions, however, are not natural phenomena in this sense but undertakings that Da-sein chooses pro-jectively within the context of its world. As Heidegger explains later in the *Seminars*, animals stand in relation to an "environment," while human beings exist in relation to their "world" (p. 244). Dwelling in a world entails "being addressed" by "beings other than {{Da-sein}}" (p. 137). In other words, being enworlded involves the "stress" of always and already encountering persons and things—of meeting "beings other than himself" (p. 137). This encountering is not a passive contiguity of self and other but an active and uniquely generative responding by Da-sein. Hence, moving toward or away as essentially human phenomena cannot be causal phenomena: "Propensity [*Neigung*] and resistance [*Abwehr*] are also modes of relationship to what is present. Psychical capacities are to be understood as modes of being addressed [*Angesprochensein*] and of responding [*Entsprechen*]" (p. 219). Even thinking of moving toward and away as emergent properties, to use a philosophical expression with some history, likely distorts Heidegger's point. While the whole may be greater than the sum of its parts, Heidegger would probably object to any focus on parts as generators of wholes (even if the wholes are not reducible to those parts). "Part talk" suggests representational thinking—the manipulative orientation that renders Da-sein's encounter with beings a pre-ordered and thus pre-judged venture. Heidegger states: "A responding can only exist when one is able to say yes or no" (p. 219). Since being able to say yes or no is a matter of language, and since articulation is integral to being in the world, we can make sense of motive only through our being in the world, and being in the world is originally and consistently a concept of Da-sein's existential wholeness. Heidegger says: "[W]hen it {{responding}} involves being urged [*Gedrängstein*], responding is devalued to a mere [external] relation" (p. 219). Furthermore: "In an urge [*Drang*], the experience of something *as* something is not explicit" (p. 219). He gives the example of a mother who is overly close to her child and how this closeness "takes on the characteristics of narrowness [*Enge*] and choking [*Erwürgen*]" to the point where "to save herself from this entanglement [*Verstrickung*] and narrowness, the child must be removed and strangled" (p. 219). Thus, we must interpret even a "pathological urge" by way of the entirety of Da-sein as being-in-the-world. While Da-sein may stray from self-understanding and devolve into "automatic" behaviors, the primacy of existentially shaped meaning remains. Responding is a personal and interpersonal phenomenon of Da-sein as a pro-jective being. We understand ourselves inaccurately and diminish the truth of our being as "sustaining a realm of openness" when we reduce receiving-perceiving to mechanism (p. 218). Emmy van Deurzen says in "Heidegger and Psychotherapy":

> The overall postulate of most forms of psychotherapy is that the individual is ill or deficient and has to be cured. Existential psychotherapy breaks the mould by insisting on not attempting to heal a person's overt distress but rather to value it as a source of covert truth (1995, pp. 18–19).

In her view, a psychotherapeutic client experiences problems with disclosure—with himself as disclosing being-in-the-world. Van Deurzen concludes: "If mental health care is to be about adjustment and cure the existential approach may not be advisable. . . . [I]t is about revitalising the human ability for truth, intensity and resolute living" (p. 24).

4. Being-with

Being and Time underscores the defining reality of interpersonal relations in Da-sein's existence. Da-sein does not dwell alone but always and already with others. Heidegger's approach heads off the Cartesian chasm of self versus other. Descartes's *Meditations* present an ego that matches up eventually with an external world (and God), but fellow egos scarcely appear. The most notable, or at least startling, mention of others is the passage in which Descartes speculates as to whether conscious beings or mere automata lie underneath the hats and coats that he sees from his window. His doubt is admittedly procedural in nature, as he declares that he will doubt the testimony of the senses generally since they have deceived him on occasion. Whatever has deceived once, he reasons, may deceive again. Descartes does not give a specific ground for doubting the reality of other conscious subjects, but insists on absolutely thoroughgoing doubt as the only way to know whether anything at all merits the blessing of critical scrutiny. Even so, his speculation strikes us as bordering on madness: Why would one doubt the reality of fellow persons?

Less strikingly, to give another example, any strong form of individualism attenuates the foundational truth of our life with others. Da-sein does not exist merely alongside others, a manner of expression that suggests being located indifferently within a collection of objects unless a cause for "interaction" arises. In truth, Da-sein dwells with others at all times, even when alone (whether by choice or force). We simply cannot make sense of Da-sein as receiving-perceiving without clear and constant reference to its world of meanings and projects as shaped by the presence of other Da-seins. We want others for their qualities and need them to secure our plans; separation from others deprives us of desired affiliation, foils our designs, and may even plunge us into despair. Choosing to stay apart from others is still a way of taking a stand on persons who concern us, if unfortunately. A global lack of deep or felt relation with others and clinical depression usually appear together. Recall as well our discussion of boredom. Even in boredom, in seemingly pure disaffectedness, we dwell in the world temporally with others. We do not want to listen to others; we feel that we will gain little or nothing by listening to them; we exist in a nullifying relation to others, yet our association can never be nullified entirely but only interpreted differently. What is near can become what is far, but never so far as to sever the basic affiliation among persons. Alienation presupposes an originative truth. Even empathy presupposes something deeper, as Lang, Brunnhuber, and Wagner explain: "'Empathy' does not first constitute Being-with; only on the basis of Being-with does 'empathy' become possible" (2003, p. 358). Though we are pro-jective beings in Heidegger's special sense of projection, we do not empathetically thrust ourselves ballistically into others as though they are objects to be entered externally through an act of will. Boss warns in *Psychoanalysis and Daseinsanalysis*:

> *Entwurf* {{projection}} and *Entschlossenheit* {{world-disclosure}}, in the sense Heidegger uses these terms, should never be, as they so often are, misunderstand to mean a 'projection' by, or the 'resoluteness' of, a {{hyper-agential}} subject (1963, p. 39).

As interpreting being-in-the-world, Da-sein understands in the first instance the being-in-the-world of others: "{{Being-with}} presuppose[s] that one has already [existentially] understood the other as another human being; otherwise, I would be projecting something into the void" (2001, p. 162).

Each physical being of the human type forms in and emerges out of another human being's body (the mother's body), after which survival and development—biological, material, cognitive, affective, intellectual, and personal—are premised on the care of others. Connectedness is inaugural and irreducible. The event of birth evinces at the same moment Da-sein's connectedness and separation. Without question, Da-sein is an individuated being. This individuation, though, emerges at the same time as deep relation. If Da-sein happens to be alone, we cannot render intelligible this aloneness except by reference to original being with others. Even the most solitary hermit is a hermit only by way of not-being-with-others. (Even Nietzsche's Zarathustra descends the mountain of his voluntary exile out of "love of man.") The concept of being apart makes sense only if we assume being together. A tension appears to exist within *Being and Time* between Da-sein's coming to itself and Da-sein's *mit-Sein*: its being-with-others. Indeed, as we will see in the next chapter, resisting the attraction of "the others" as "average" persons is a condition of becoming one's own Da-sein. Da-sein must withstand the enticement of the everyday or mundane attitudes and comportments that average humanity prescribes. We can see the beginning of a solution, though, in the phrasing here. Heidegger says that Da-sein must overcome its tendency to fall headlong into the mere ordinariness of social life, not that it should—or even can—deny the reality of social life or the extraordinary possibilities of human relation that lie within this sphere. Da-sein must continue its habitation with other Da-seins while seeking a more fitting appropriation of its defining possibilities, and all variations in Da-sein's relations with others, from the marketplace to the hermitage, derive their comprehensibility from this primitive togetherness.

A large number—the preponderance—of psychotherapeutic issues concern relations with others, and the relation between the client and the psychotherapeutic practitioner is itself a living instance of being-with. Leaving aside the possibility of performing psychological procedures on oneself, all psychotherapy falls within the purview of interpersonal relations. As Boss suggests, the more the practitioner is attuned to being-with, the better the therapy: Preconceptions thwart the fullness of being-with by shrinking the client into simplistic objecthood, into a function of some theoretical apparatus. Ernesto Spinelli says in *Demystifying Therapy*:

> It would surprising, . . . for most of us not to assume such things as the existence of an 'unconscious' mind, or to disavow the notion that experiences and 'traumas' from an individual's infancy and childhood provide the key to the understanding of his or her adult personality. We speak authoritatively, if not glibly, about *archetypal* individuals such as 'the archetypal' hero, sex goddess, or football player; we recognize the hidden (often erotic or aggressive) meanings of all manner of symbolic images and verbal allusions employed by novelists, film directors and advertising agencies; we would find it surprising if one were to suggest that each of us does not harbour seemingly forgotten (or repressed) memories which, nevertheless, continue to exert their psychic hold upon us (1994, pp. 12–13).

His "existential-phenomenological" vision of psychotherapy emphasizes the "being qualities" of the therapist: the inevitable sway of the person of the therapist (p. 15). Spinelli warns us away firmly from conceptual contrivances, technical tricks, and micro-political machinations, and instead offers sketches of the therapist as a non-authoritarian fellow inquirer who is both "with" and "for" the client. Anything less and we are stuck with, on my understanding of his perspective, some level of fettered thinking and feeling, sadomasochism, compromised critical engagement, and what we can call simply "poor being." Alex Howard says in *Philosophy for Counselling and Psychotherapy*:

> Heidegger's view was that Joe Average would be most keen to be led by the counsellor, or any other authority figure, to be told, implicitly or explicitly, who they were, what they were, how to talk and think about themselves, where to go, what to do (2000, p. 335).

Heidegger says in the *Seminars*:

> Since one can [supposedly] only do therapy, which is a concerned handling of objects, and thus something purely technical, then the outcome of such psychotherapy cannot result in a healthier human being. In such a therapy, the human being is finally eliminated. At best, such a therapy could [only] result in a more polished object (2001, p. 215).

Louis S. Berger distinguishes in *Psychotherapy as Praxis: Abandoning Misapplied Science* "the technotherapies . . . identified with Cartesianism and natural science, and the praxis-based psychotherapies {{associated}} with Cartesianism's 'other'" (2002, p. 4). Spinelli says: "Some clues from research studies suggest that its {{the therapeutic relationship's}} importance and uniqueness lie in the therapist's willingness to listen to and 'be with' the client" (1994, p. 287). He hastens to add that "these terms also remain somewhat vague, and if they are to be helpful they must be clarified further", and proceeds to distinguish (among other elements) being-with and being-for the client. In embodying being-with, the therapist "*stays with the experienced truths of the client as they are being related* in order that they, and whatever implications such truths may hold, be exposed to further investigation and clarification" (p. 297, p. 315). Being-with here means a "willingness to *acknowledge the lived reality of the client,* . . ." (p. 315). Being-for clients aims "*to seek to keep up with them side by side*" so that the worlds of the client and the therapist are sufficiently congruent (p. 317). Thus, being-for is a matter of "*attempt[ing] to enter the client's lived reality*": of trying to experience the client's "way of being" (p. 317). We might be tempted to think of being-with as passive and of being-for as active, but both are active. Acknowledging the client's experience is a decision, an act, and a steadfast receptivity, and is by no means assumed or automatic. (People fail or refuse to acknowledge the experience of others all the time.) Entering the client's experience—which is similar to Heidegger's "leaping ahead," as we will see—is also a decision, act, and persevering willingness. Focusing on the "being qualities" in the therapeutic situation "subverts the possibility of the therapist's task being that of 'truth bringer', 'healer' or 'helper' in any purposive or direct manner" (p. 317). The client may well interpret the therapist in such a fashion, Spinelli admits, but the therapist must resist any interpersonal or inner call to perform as an "authority," a stance that undermines the co-sojourning of the two beings-in-the-world who form the therapeutic relationship. Furthermore, "doing qualities" alone—skills, techniques, and "expertise" by themselves—are inadequate to found a fully productive therapeutic relationship, he argues, since "being qualities" comprise the crux of the client-therapist relation. Skills, techniques, and expertise, when applied appropriately, surely contribute to therapeutic efficacy (as Spinelli is happy to admit), but they can become compromised, if well intentioned, responses on the part of the therapist when some insufficiency in or incongruence concerning "being qualities" exists. Heidegger says in the *Seminars*: "Any adjustment [by the patient] is only possible and meaningful on the ground of existential being-with [*Mitsein*]" (2001, p. 157). We will return to the question of "being qualities" when we discuss Daseinsanalysis.

5. Bodying Forth

We broached in the Introduction Heidegger's work on the body. We should now return to this matter to achieve a broader grasp of his account of Da-sein. We may begin by recounting an instance of dialog between Heidegger and one of the seminar participants regarding space (this passage also elucidates our points above about the nature of understanding):

> MH {{Martin Heidegger}}: Let's assume you close your eyes. When you open them again, is the table gone? What then?
> SP {{Seminar participant}}: Amazement, disappointment.
> MH: What does disappointment mean?
> SP: An unfulfilled expectation.
> MH: Yes, exactly. Even when your eyes were closed, you were by the table. Dr. R. then perceives the table here from over there. How does this happen? Then where is R.?
> SP: Here and there.
> MH: R. is here and there at the same time, but the table cannot be here and there at the same time. Only the human being can be here and there at the same time. The table is in space in a different way than the human being (p. 11).

Da-sein can *be* both "here" and "there" precisely and only because it is being t/here: being-in-the-world as pro-jective ek-isting. As well, animals do not "experience space *as space*" (p. 16). Heidegger uses the word *Entwurf* to indicate Da-sein's "throwing" of itself and possibilities: We venture ourselves into the world and future by choosing amongst possibilities, thus creating our own ways of being in the world. Most translators render this word as projection. The table that can be in only one spot—unlike, phenomenologically speaking, the human being—"has been arranged in the room. It is oriented according to a way of living" (p. 13). The arranging of the table in the room serves a human purpose; even though it is a physical object, it evinces a pro-jective meaning. Space, then, *for* the human being, is not a container, an emptiness, or just a non-human physical reality—its spatiality "consists of its being pervious, its being open, and its being a free [realm]" (p. 8). Space is not itself spatial, on this reasoning. Space, *for us*, is a matter of being situated in this way or that way, but being situated is a phenomenological-hermeneutic category, not an "objective" physical one. Indeed, Heidegger claims explicitly: "What is in space is grounded on the open and on the free"—on the *Da*, in other words (p. 8). (He also says that the void assumes the open and the free.) What space is for us, our understanding of it, depends upon our comportment. For example, as Heidegger remarks: "A wall can be put between the observer and the table. Then space is no longer pervious to seeing the table but is open for building a wall. Without its openness, a wall could not be built between them" (p. 8). Da-sein's bodying forth cannot be understood essentially through the concepts of physical science. Our body is obviously physical, and it is subject to investigation and manipulation by science, but our bodily existence in its richness is not reducible to scientifically verifiable phenomena. Scientific or quasi-scientific views develop within Da-sein's dwelling and bodying forth, but they can never ground dwelling and bodying forth. *Soma* as an aspect of Da-sein's being-in-the-world cannot be claimed, or claimed entirely, by physical approaches.

We should consider, Heidegger suggests, the case of Galileo. What is the space of nature (the nature of space) for Galileo? Heidegger says:

> As a natural scientific observer, Galileo disregarded the tree, the apple, and the ground in observing the fall of the apple. He saw only a point of mass falling from one location in space to another location in space in law-governed fashion (p. 30).

Descartes also construes space as extension, but the approaches of Descartes and Galileo do not address the question of what space is for Da-sein as being t/here spatially. Naturalistic approaches that masquerade as phenomenological manifestation are ironic involuntarily, for "[n]o one can experiment with these [a priori] assumptions" (p. 28). Such orientations lack a proper connection to Da-sein's receiving-perceiving. What is space "itself"? Space, as the "medium" of our bodies and all physical things, "exists" everywhere—or does it? Heidegger makes the following phenomenological point: "When we observe the cup, we receive-perceive that space, spaceness . . . surrounds the cup and grants its place, but we *never* perceive what space itself is" (p. 32). Space is not for us as receivers-perceivers essentially a medium in which our bodies and other things are inserted or arranged mechanically, and space does not exist as we exist. We settle for an abstract and reified sense of space and perceptual phenomena only when we lose touch with the primordial in-ness of our being in the world: "I always hear the motorcycle, the call of the church bell first. It requires a very artificial approach to be able to distill a pure sensory datum from what was heard" (p. 142). Hersch emphasizes "the experiential whole that comes first; its distinguishable elements are elaborated secondarily and abstractly" (p. 69). Contrast the dissociated protagonist of Fernando Pessoa's *The Book of Disquiet*, the title of which bespeaks his abnormal frame and calls to mind Jean-Paul Sartre's *Nausea*: "Voices emerge not from people's throats but from the air itself" (1991, p. 35). To speak more scientifically for the sake of naturalists, but with a core of phenomenological truth: "The *psyche* does not exist as something separate from the body, but pervades the whole organism" (2001, p. 78). Gendlin says in *Experiencing and the Creation of Meaning*:

> It is *impossible to isolate the units in the body, except* if a specific and limited point of view is taken. From a given point of view certain systems or organs or cellular processes can be studied as units, but even a slight shift in point of view will require different modes of isolating units.
>
> In some respects the body is one interpenetrating system in which every aspect of order involves every other aspect. In other words, one can divide, but only with respect to some one limited point of view, which one will have to forego for other respects (1962, p. 25).

Da-sein's basic orientation in the world, its receiving-perceiving, is not merely physical or mental or an assemblage of the two (if such an arrangement were even possible)—it is a whole way of sensing, acting, deciding, and thinking.

We may use gesture as an illustration of this holism. Gestures, as overt bodily and spatial events, may be measured and analyzed scientifically (at least to some extent), but scientific probing cannot provide a comprehensive account of gesture. Gesture is a phenomenon of the human being as active being-in-the-world, laden with pro-jective meaning. Heidegger calls gesture "gathered . . . bearing and comportment" (2001, p. 91). This gathering in receiving-perceiving does not occur in an abstract, barren space—the space of the impersonal scientific-naturalistic universe. It happens in the space of Da-sein's sojourning in the world:

> Each movement of my body as a "gesture" and, therefore, as such and such a comportment does not simply enter into an indifferent space. Rather, comportment is always already in a certain region . . . which is open and through the thing to which I am in a relationship, . . . (p. 91).

Heidegger adds swiftly that gesturing (in most cases) is also a phenomenon of being-with: We gesture as part of making our way in the world in concrete situations with others. Blushing that bears a social aspect is another example of bodying forth as being-in-the-world. Some instances of blushing occur involuntarily following changes of internal or external temperature, but in other cases blushing expresses diffidence or shame. In any event, Heidegger says, blushing takes different forms but they "are immediately distinguished in our everyday being-with and being-for each other. We can 'see' from the respective situations whether someone is embarrassed, for instance, or flushed for some other reason" (p. 81). Analyzing quantitatively and separating out explanatorily the flow of blood in a person's face cannot stand as a faithful reckoning of the phenomenon of blushing. We need to discern the truth of Da-sein's enworlded bodying forth to understand both blushing and gesturing. A strictly naturalistic account is insufficient. What, to use another example, are the spatial limits of a person's body? The obvious answer is that a body's empirically ascertainable dimensions comprise its spatial limits. Such dimensions are almost completely available to the naked eye. Now Heidegger argues that the "bodily limit"—the "shape" of Da-sein's bodying forth—is not identical to the "corporeal limit"—the overtly physical body: "When pointing with my finger toward the crossbar of the window over there, I [as body] do not end at my fingertips" (p. 86). Thus, *the bodily limit is extended beyond the corporeal limit*" (p. 86). For example, it should be clear that embracing another person "in space" is not simply a matter of two objects coming into physical contact in a measurable manner. Heidegger says: "The physiological dimension is a necessary condition for the possibility of a relationship between one human being and another. . . . {{Yet}} no sense organ exists for what is called 'the other' . . ." (p. 155). Da-sein's space, then, is not exclusively the space of natural science but in the first instance the openness of being in the world projectively with other "whos" and things ("objects"). This is a basic phenomenological and hermeneutic point; indeed, it is a point of common sense. Heidegger uses the example of a foreign "tribesman" who encounters a watch (chronometer) to show the plain truth of Da-sein's situatedness:

> The thing is not a watch for him, and so it is not an indicator of time {{as it us for us given our pro-jective meanings}}. Of course, this does not mean that the relationship to time is foreign to this human being. Presumably, he lives in a more original relationship to time than we modern Europeans, who recommend our strange products to him (p. 39).

We can, in keeping with our emphasis here, extend this example by imagining, say, exposure to a sextant, a device that such a person would find unintelligible, or simply unnecessary owing to other means of achieving similar ends.

Heidegger spends much of his energy on the question of time. How does Da-sein as bodily receiving-perceiving exist as a being "in" time? How do Da-sein and time belong together bodily—"the belonging together of time and the human being's unfolding essence"? (p. 38). The example about a tribesman and a watch shows that devices are not necessary for us to dwell temporally. We always and already sojourn through time: "Even when the clock has stopped, time does not disappear at all. I am just unable to tell what time it is" (p. 29). Our eyes do not need to see a clock or a watch to experience time. While we all have a sense of time, we do not usually reflect on the nature of our lived time. We pro-ject a past, a present, and a future, but we do not normally "thematize" these temporal dimensions. Thematization is the process of attending explicitly to a phenomenon or an aspect of a phenomenon that is normally ground rather than figure, to use the nomenclature of Gestalt psychology. Pursuing the nature of time or space does not leave us with mere abstractions: "We merely make something thematic that was concomitantly given . . . as unthematic and necessary" (p. 32). We cannot, however, divorce time or space from their "contents"; fidelity demands that we attend to the entirety of the phenomenological situation. As Heidegger says: "I determine every 'now' as *related to something*" (p. 34).

Heidegger indicates now-ness as the initial feature of our experience of time. This now-ness shows the sequential character of time: "All 'nows' are one after another" (p. 34). Nows are singular and exclusive, unlike the points of space, which exist simultaneously (p. 34). Nonetheless, they are connected ultimately; Heidegger uses the word "span" (a word with a physical sense) to describe this connectedness. If nows are exclusive, how can they be connected, and how can spanning happen? Heidegger says of our immediate experience of time: "Each now we say is simultaneously also 'just now' and 'at once,' that is, the time we have addressed with the word 'now' has a *span*. In itself every 'now' is still also a 'just now' and an 'at once'" (p. 34). Thus, spanning is the central feature of Da-sein's experience of time. The "just now" becomes eventually the past; the "at once" becomes eventually the future. The word spanning expresses the incipient unfolding, backwards and forwards, of otherwise singular nows. Heidegger construes original now-ness as an experience that stands apart from the regularized nows of clock time: "Counting time is a specific comportment to time in which the characteristics of being spanned toward 'just now' and toward 'at once' are no longer noticed" (p. 34). The now becomes an instant in a series of instants; the lived experience of the incipient unfolding of nows backwards into the past—"no-longer-being"—and future—"not-yet-being"—withers (p. 35). Heidegger's concern is not to declare clock time invalid but simply to show how the measurement of time changes the manner in which Da-sein experiences time—in which Da-sein dwells as time. He defines memory as "a retaining of something-which-has-been [*Gewesenes*] in the world in the standing-open of human existence" (p.

202). Heidegger's use of the word "retaining" is, however, ambivalent deliberately. He admits the reality and usefulness of the concept but hastens to locate it in the more original ground of Da-sein's standing-open. Heidegger says: "Insofar as the human being is a bodying forth, it cannot be denied that something happens in the brain which is observable in the physical body [*Leibkörper*]" (p. 202). At the same time, he claims, "remembering cannot be grasped by the method of natural science. Only the bodily-corporeal [*leib-körperlich*] conditions of its performance can be ascertained" (p. 202). Remembering as a subject of natural science, Heidegger opines, presupposes a "storage" of "things," yet being-in-the-world as receiving-perceiving is not a container and memories are not object-units. Heidegger asserts that physical factors are "merely *conditions* for the emergence of the phenomenon" and "not *causes*, and surely not memory itself" (p. 202). The phenomenon of remembering as Da-sein lives it is ek-static being-in and being-with: the vital intertwining of the meanings of past, present, and future. Instead of capturing being-in-the-world in a grid of calculability, Da-sein's ek-sistence as a time-ly being who moves pro-jectively through the physical realm shows the derivativeness of the notion of external calculability. Just as time is not a set of identical nows, bodily being—"being-in-space"—is not a matter of mechanism for being t/here as receiving-perceiving who bodies forth pro-jectively. The spanning of Da-sein as time holds true as well for Da-sein as bodying forth: We ek-sist here and there at once. As Heidegger says, "our being-here with things is always already a being-there with distant things not physically present, even if these things are not meant and made-present explicitly" (p. 73). We are a coming from . . . and a going to . . . . This bodily spanning is possible only because "the body" is not physical: "There is actually no phenomenology of the body because the body is not a corporeal thing [*Körper*]" (p. 184). How can the body not be a corporeal thing? It is evidently so in one sense—the sense of natural science—but it is not so in the phenomenological-hermeneutic sense that Heidegger develops in the *Seminars*. Bodying forth is one of the central features of being t/here in the world; it is an open prospect for Da-sein's projective engagements and meanings. Bodying forth is a dynamic and highly intricate expanse of "heres" and "theres" through which Da-sein sojourns as it does:

> Bodily being [*das Leibliche*] is founded upon responding [*Entsprechen*] [to a world]. Bodily being is *not* first something present for itself [as a subject] through which a relationship-current [*Bezugstrom*] is then transmitted, like a current transmitted through the hand. The body is the necessary condition, but not a sufficient condition, for the relationship . . . . The phenomenon of the body is wholly unique and irreducible to something else, for instance, irreducible to mechanistic systems (p. 186).

As being-in the-world, Da-sein's bodily reality is an "understanding-of-being" (p. 200). Even a condition such as aphasia that we take to be wholly physical is an understanding-of-being: "A bodying forth . . . co-participates in the receiving-perceiving of what is present, even if it is addressed silently. . . . For an aphasic person can indeed say what he means, but he cannot utter it out loud" (p. 200). The texture of human experience as bodying forth is meaningful in the first instance. The "lack of a tongue" in the case of an aphasic does not mean that the person has ceased to body forth meaningfully (p. 200). This Da-sein is still an articulating being who, as she is able, lets things show themselves. The aphasic human being remains an understanding and interpreting un/concealment, even if, from one perspective, she is a compromised one. Her human character does not disappear with the disappearance or attenuation of her aptitude for overt verbal articulation—else articulation is the merely calculative use of language. While we use language for "calculating" purposes, articulation, in Heidegger's view, is a broader feature of Da-sein's constitution. Being t/here's meaningful receiving-perceiving, its standing open understandingly in being, *is* articulation, and founds the narrower concept of "language."

The body as a physical object of natural science exists, but it does not eksist. Da-sein ek-sists. Being-in-the-world is the sway of the human being as a pro-jective clearing in being. The body as gross matter is visible, but bodying forth through the world is invisible: It is a meaningful responding that is freighted with pro-jective understandings. A person cannot live without a body, yet taking the body as gross matter to be the fundamental category of our life is a blunder. Existing is the defining feature of the human kind of being:

> Then everything we call our bodiliness, down to the last muscle fiber and down to the most hidden molecule of hormone, belongs essentially to existing. Thus, it is basically *not* inanimate matter but a domain of that nonobjectifiable, optically invisible capacity to receive-perceive the significance of what it encounters, which constitutes the whole Da-sein. {{The bodily spheres of existing}} cannot be cared for in a toolbox. Rather, they remain in the sway of being human, held in it, and belonging to it so long as the human being lives (p. 232).

Heidegger acknowledges readily that we regard our own bodies as grossly material and mechanical all the time—otherwise, how could we maneuver through a world of physical objects?—but remains adamant that such uses and interpretations always and already presuppose the more elemental sway of "being human."

Part Two

WAYS OF BEING

Three

DA-SEIN AS POSSIBILITY

1. Being Called and Falling

We are called into openness, a task that demands reticence—holding thoughtfully to the revealing-concealing that we are. We fall into forgetfulness, however, allowing ourselves to become absorbed into the perceived comfort of idle talk, curiosity, and ambiguity. Let us reverse the order in *Being and Time* and consider first ambiguity. Heidegger's treatment of ambiguity forms part of his more general investigation of the "falling" of Da-sein: "The Everyday Being of the 'There'" as the "they-self" (1962, p. 210). The "they-self"—*das Man*, or "the one"—is Da-sein inasmuch as it is dispersed into the thoughtlessness of depersonalization. The "one" of the they-self is no one in particular. Heidegger's definition of ambiguity is crucial to our comprehension of self and other yet it is not easy to grasp:

> When, in our everyday Being-with-one-another, we encounter the sort of thing which is accessible to everyone, and about which anyone can say anything, it soon becomes impossible to decide what is disclosed in a genuine understanding, and what is not (p. 217).

That which is accessible to everyone and about which anyone can say anything appears as amorphous, as lacking full form. This lack allows Da-sein, individually and collectively, the possibility of lying fallow. In truth, Da-sein exists in its world only definitely and never abstractly, but when Da-sein seizes upon the ambiguous in this fashion it converts shapelessness into a putative virtue and a primary feature of human existing. Da-sein thereby loses "genuine understanding" and gains the false security of an inferior understanding. This sham knowledge spares Da-sein the work of thinking through and transfiguring its existence, and enables Da-sein to persist in refusal of its ownmost possibilities. Therefore, ambiguity plays a central role epistemically in Da-sein's being in the world: Da-sein indeed grasps its basic reality but in the first general instance only through the leveling filter of the amorphousness of they-being. Da-sein's knowing bears the imprint of its original absorption into distractedness that avoids chronically a deep appropriation of sojourning's essential possibilities and responsibilities. Beauvoir articulates sharply the primal nature of decision in *The Blood of Others*: "A single word—and the thing will exist, it will never cease to exist. A rap on the door, a word, and time is cleft asunder, divided into two fragments which can never again be united" (1964,

p. 34). Heidegger describes ambiguity as "noncommittal just-guessing-with-someone" (1992, p. 162). We see in this definition the element of refusal of decisive action and the necessity of generic others to corroborate the validity of the "here-and-there" spottiness (rather than the "t/here" truth) of what is allegedly known with sureness.

Idle talk and curiosity are of a piece with ambiguity; these three realities comprise co-phenomena of our everyday being in the world. Idle talk is, in plain terms, chattering about nothing much. We could also call it gossiping, as Heidegger does at points, though his definition of idle talk is broader than gossiping in the usual sense. Chattering (together) about nothing much characterizes truly our ordinary dwelling, on his view. It is merely "average intelligibility" (1962, p. 212). Idle talk proceeds from "nowhere" and "no one" and leads no "where" and to no "one." The "one" of idle talk is the they-self. Prating is an occlusion of the essential "t/here" and "who" of Da-sein's being, which is always a particular existing. The character in Samuel Beckett's *The Unnamable* says: "What doesn't come to me from me has come to the wrong address" (1997, p. 400). He continues:

> Between them they find a rejoinder to everything. And how they enjoy talking, they know there is no worse torment, for one not in the conversation. They are numerous, all round, holding hands perhaps, an endless chain, taking turns to talk. They wheel, in jerks, so that the voice always comes from the same quarter. But often they all speak at once, they all say simultaneously the same thing exactly, but so perfectly together that one would take it for a single voice, a single mouth, . . . (p. 407).

> Who would ever think, to hear me, that I've never seen anything, never heard anything but their voices? (p. 369).

Idle talk, then, as an exaggeration and exploitation of shapelessness, is a concealment of the reality of Da-sein's being. This indistinctness enables Da-sein to twist arbitrarily its own truths into self-satisfying bromides. While idle talk is an "uprooting" that allows Da-sein to stay "floating unattached," Da-sein "*is* its 'there', its 'in-the-world'" (1962, p. 214). Idle talk is itself part of Da-sein's reality—a truth that comprises not just revealing but concealing. As Heidegger says: "The fact that something has been said groundlessly, and then gets passed along in further retelling, amounts to perverting the act of disclosing into an act of closing off" (p. 213). Idle talk is not "*consciously passing off* something as something else"; its stubbornness and danger, rather, lie precisely in the complexly attenuated nature of its appearing (p. 213). Richardson, speaking of Lacan, distinguishes "empty speech"—a "talking in vain"—and "full speech," which is "revelatory in nature and takes place when meaning (sense) is discovered in an historicizing process" (2003, p. 90). He adds:

"Founded thus in language itself, truth has an inexhaustible resilience" (p. 90). Richardson recalls Heidegger's conception of a-lethic truth: "originary truth as e-vidence/discovery/disclosure"—as letting come to be in full speech, on the understanding that "full" speech lies open always to further hermeneutic interpretation (p. 94).

Curiosity completes this triad of existential digressions. We are curious when we see *"just* in order to see" rather than to understand, Heidegger says (1962, p. 216). He elaborates: "It {{curious experiencing}} seeks novelty only in order to leap from it anew to another novelty" (p. 216). As he also expresses the point: Da-sein chooses "abandoning itself to the world" (p. 216). Tabloid media, most television and film, much music, and an appreciable portion of the Internet fall into this category of trivial distraction; idle talk, as an accomplice of curiosity, "says what one 'must' have read and seen" (p. 217). (The rise of technology did not create curiosity, but contemporary technology facilitates Da-sein's fascination with novelty.) We should not mistake Heidegger for a dour ascetic. He speaks approvingly of "marvelling" (p. 216). What could be richer than a call for ek-static understanding—for wisdom? We must grant that curiosity is a kind of understanding, but add immediately that it is a sort of comprehension which knows "just in order to have known" (p. 217). This seeking of novelty constitutes paradoxically an acquisitiveness of the dispensable. Kierkegaard speaks relentlessly against this tendency.

Ambiguity, idle talk, and curiosity are phenomena of the they-self, which is Da-sein's everyday self; *"as a primordial phenomenon, it belongs to Da-sein's positive constitution"* (p. 167). In other words, as Heidegger says, no sense exists in decrying the they-self as an unreal or accidental self; they-ness just *is* Da-sein's average way of being in the world. They-ness is not a tag-along identity, but our normal mode of dwelling. It expresses being-in-the-world's heedless absorption into the world, and thus Da-sein's falling away from its most intimate possibilities for existing. Heidegger characterizes this narcotizing assimilation into ambiguity as dispersion. We spread ourselves out in pursuit of an abeyance of identity, but the fundamental reality of our being-in-the-world and its claim upon us is unavoidable. Heidegger also uses the terms "distantiality {{distance from one's ownmost self}}, averageness, and levelling down" to describe the "publicness" of the they-self (p. 165). As he elaborates:

> [I]t prescribes what can and may be ventured, . . . Every kind of priority gets noiselessly suppressed. Overnight, everything that is primordial gets glossed over as something that has long been well known. Everything gained by a struggle becomes just something to be manipulated. Every secret loses its force (p. 165).

The they-self, as the average everyday identity of Da-sein, dilutes and chokes off vital concerns of existence. Average everyday understanding, at its worst, is "sham clarity—the unintelligibility of the trivial" (p. 208). Heidegger says in the *Seminars*: "Leveling down is a kind of privation. . . . Where everything is uniformly accessible to everyone indiscriminately, all elimination of difference in rank is at work" (2001, p. 50). Even if the privation is extensive, "void" is grounded in freedom—the freedom of Da-sein as a kinetic opening who responds to the interrogatory call of being (pp. 14–15).

While the phenomenon of the they-self is a general aspect of Da-sein's existing as an enworlded being, it can occur only in localized ways. Da-sein always dwells in and through some chosen assemblage of projects. As being-with, Da-sein lives in the company of others. Thus, Da-sein's engaged particularity includes others, who also bear their own undertakings. The existences of Da-sein and other cohere most clearly when a definite interest claims both, when they find themselves sharing the same sub-cultural ethos, such as the "world" of business or the "world" of art. The dispersion of the individual self into an ambiguous they-self transpires regardless of the perceived or intended features of the sub-cultural ethos at issue, regardless of its allegedly neutral, transcendental, or liberating nature. All are ensnared in the thicket of conformism, mandatory discourse, and engrossment with ever-new "developments." They-selfness informs local context, whether the context is simple or complex. We must be plain about the global reality of this phenomenon: Technical, intellectual, or any other sort of sophistication cannot eradicate this primitive structure of Da-sein's existing. The tendency toward a cacophonous scattering of self, a "pulling apart" of this living instance of being in the world, is inexorable. Da-sein attains an ironic safety in depersonalization, and apparently exquisite individuation is no remedy. For example, academics, who are highly educated, uncommonly articulate, and devoted (ostensibly) to unriddling the cosmos, suffer no less from the pull of their localized they-selfness than do humbler mortals in any other sub-cultural ethos. Indeed, the falling of academics proves all the more instructive because of their supposedly privileged vantage. The human condition pervades all levels and concoctions. The norm of the "company" academic, consecrated ways of speaking and writing, and a mania for incessant but suspect "advances" besot academe despite its airs of progressiveness. (The fact that the activities of academe are generally better undertaken in human life than not undertaken is not the point; the moral, rather, is that what passes for enlightenment is often shockingly dim.)

In any case, the phenomenon of the they-self entails a will to reject or shrink whatever compromises the apparent security of the they-self. Anything that threatens the prized floating quality of depersonalized personhood is fit for suppression, diminution, and even persecution. Leon Festinger's theory of cognitive dissonance is germane. It holds that cognitive discrepancies (for instance, between what we believe at the moment and new but contrary information) cause us discomfort and that we are inclined often to lessen such divergences by irrational means (say, by figuring without grounds that the new but contrary information must be faulty). Distance from self by way of absorption into an "other" self that is neither here nor there, the easy route of majoritarianism, and the squashing of impertinent questions are ways in which Da-sein as they-self enforces a regime of artificial regularity. As they-self, Da-sein loses sight of its truth as t/here: as an enworlded being who, while always existing with others, must depend on its own thoughtful appropriative activity for meaning. Da-sein is "there" in its world as a standing-out in the midst of beings and "here" as the concrete agent of its world of particular concerns. Both the "there" of standing out, of existing at all, and the ceaseless "here" of being in a situation call for genuine recognition of being in the world in all its fullness and implications. Da-sein is called and claimed elementally by (its own) being. This summons usually provokes dismay, as being is a mystery, a mixture of the known, the unknown, and the unknowable, an enigmatic truth that most people would prefer to simplify. Spinelli says: "All sedimented beliefs, attitudes, rules, certainties must be forsaken in favour of disquieting uncertainty" (1989, p. 112). He explains that, as engaged being-in-the-world, Da-sein must naturally embody beliefs and attitudes of some stripe, but that at the same time "we must acknowledge them as being just that—beliefs, or suppositions, that we might choose to live our lives by" (p. 112). Heidegger says in the *Seminars*:

> The human being is essentially in need of help because he is always in danger of losing himself and of not coming to grips with himself. This danger is connected with the human being's freedom. The entire question of the human being's capacity for being ill is connected with the imperfection of his unfolding essence. Each illness is a loss of freedom, a constriction of the possibility for living (2001, p. 157).

The willful mystifications that Da-sein invents to explain the world—grandiose myths and superstitions, arbitrary but comforting structures of belief, and unfounded or merely anthropocentric theories—fall short of an appreciation of this complexity, and embody a fear of being in the world as both a question or a call and a response. Being in the world is real yet a slipping away into . . . . Only the call of conscience can prompt Da-sein to attend more assiduously to the vital concerns of its existence, to its ownmostness as being-in-the-world. Da-sein can be what it is for the most part in its everyday life, or it can be more fully itself. This is the freedom of Da-sein as a kinetic opening. Human being as an expanse of freedom offers the possibility of becoming absorbed into . . . to the point of losing sight of the abiding and unfolding "mineness" of each Da-sein—but it also offers the possibility of recovering this mineness from the scatter of average everydayness.

We must not, however, elevate mineness into a "pure" or transcendental possibility, some sort of immaculate subjectivity or subjectivism:

> Possibilities, the possibilities of Dasein, are not a subject's tendencies or capacities. They always result, so to say, only from "outside," that is, from the particular historical situation of being-able-to-comport-oneself and of choosing, from the comportment toward what is encountered (p. 158).

Da-sein responds in this fashion or in that fashion to the address of what presents itself, and so its freedom is a "not": Choosing demands foregoing this in favor of that. This, not that, becomes what Da-sein is. We should emphasize less Da-sein's power to choose and emphasize more its choosing as a thrown throwing that *responds* as a receiving-perceiving—as an opening—in the midst of a world of others and things. While the power to choose and to effect change is an ineradicable and hugely important constituent of being-in-the-world, and while Da-sein is responsible for itself, Heidegger steers clear of any notion of a will-ful agent who imposes meaning and order on a passive (or resistant) reality "out there." An "out there" indeed exists, but it is not a mere mass of items to be regimented or subjugated. Da-sein's "out there" is the world in which it is engaged intimately and that addresses constantly Da-sein as a care-ful being whose kinesis is a responding or orienting to . . . . Da-sein may make (particular) claims for itself and on its world, but in the end *it is claimed* by its being:

> Da-sein must always be seen as being-in-the-world, as concern for things, and as caring for other [Da-seins], as the being-with the human beings it encounters, and never as a self-contained subject. Furthermore, Dasein must always be understood as standing-within [*Inne-stehen*] the clearing, . . as disclosure for what concerns it and what is encountered. At the same time *sojourn* is always comportment to [*Verhalten zu*]. . . . The "oneself" in *comporting oneself* and the "my" in "my Dasein" must never be understood as a relationship to a subject or a substance (p. 159).

Da-sein's moment by moment ek-static pro-jection towards . . . in response to the claim of what it encounters exhausts its identity. The human being *is* her dynamic and historically meaningful encounters with self, others, and things—and nothing else besides. No "essence" lies beneath or beyond this primitive reality. The human being's identity lies exactly in her being t/here as an opening, a reality in which she partakes and which grants her the possibilities of her sojourning. Thus, Heidegger cautions us:

One cannot ask about this comportment's "porter," rather the comportment carries itself. This is precisely what is wonderful about it. "Who" I am now can be said only throughout this sojourn, and always at the same time in the sojourn lies that with which and with whom I sojourn, and how I comport myself toward [them] (p. 160).

Da-sein's comportment has no "porter"—no carrier underneath the actions, no agent split off from her oriented movements, whether "internal" or overt. As one of the character's in Beauvoir's novel *The Blood of Others* says to himself in a shock of self-recognition on a battlefield: "'It's me,' he thought one day, stupefied, as he lay on the edge of a wood with a gun in his hands, . . . 'It's I who am killing them'" (1964, pp. 183-184).We *are* our comportment, which is the open range of possible ways of being-toward . . . that being in existence allows us. Boss says in *Psychoanalysis and Daseinsanalysis*:

> He {{Da-sein}} *is* at any given moment nothing but *in* and *as* this or that perceiving, instinctual, impulsive, emotional, imaginative, dreaming, thinking, acting, willing, or wishing relationship toward the things he encounters. . . . He *is* there with the particular being he encounters, even if he perceives it as being very remote from him (1963, pp. 33–34).

If being-in-the-world is its comportment, however, how can we ever be at odds with ourselves or somehow fall short of "full" identity? If Da-sein is its comportment and nothing else besides, how can it neglect or forget its own self—the claim of its own being-in-the-world as such?

2. Being Claimed, Authenticity, and Inauthenticity

What is being-in-the-world's claim upon us? What are these "vital concerns of existence"? How are we called? Da-sein is summoned—summons itself—to gather together thoughtfully and appropriate—make its own—the most decisive possibilities of its temporal-historical ek-isting. Radical decision is lost in average everydayness unless Da-sein allows the full sway of its being-in-the-world to deepen and transform its concrete activity. This means that Da-sein must marvel at its very being (in the world). We might wonder, though, whether radical decision is too strong a turn of speech, whether it panders to a stereotype of existentialism as a self-indulgent and frivolous glorification of neurotic churning and inflated gestures, and perhaps even ironically the "turbulence" of which Heidegger speaks in *Being and Time* in relation to the nature of falling (1962, p. 223). After all, most things in life do not bear extraordinary import (for example, whether to eat one vegetable or another with dinner, or whether to adopt one view or another about a new television program). Indeed, human life would not be intelligible if all meaning were to collapse into the category of the extraordinary. The word radical, however, means root, and so radical decision is resoluteness regarding matters of basic importance. We can state sensibly the cardinal need for decision about basic matters of concern while admitting that other affairs also require choice. Kierkegaard, for instance, gives an example of a basic concern that is commonplace yet profound at the same time: marriage (or, if one prefers a common contemporary expression, "being in a serious relationship"). Being married presupposes staying married, which demands, in effect, a daily re-commitment to the other person. Continual assent is implied, though at any point, of course, one might decide not to assent any longer. The idea is that being married is a definite and highly meaningful way of being in the world—yet one might lose sight of its momentousness and fall into the lassitude of an ambiguity-laden understanding of one's self and the other. Heidegger's most famous example of radical decision is death. We will all die, and we all know that we will die, but, on his analysis, we shrink from this existential truth in its fullness, preferring only a muted acknowledgment that relieves for the nonce the ubiquitous pressure of temporally constrained decision. As Kierkegaard says: "{{What if}} I had forgotten to understand what will happen to me and to every human being sometime—sometime, but what am I saying! Suppose death were insidious enough to come tomorrow!" (1992, p. 166). We may decide to treat death as an "objective" fact or inevitability, but its status as an existential "fact" means that death could not be more personal and passionately thought provoking. Mills says that authenticity is "a uniquely temporal structure and a process of unfolding possibility" (2003, p. 117). Since authenticity is "the process of becoming one's possibilities and {{is}} by nature ... idiosyncratic and uniquely subjective," paying heed to the call to authenticity is "a key therapeutic endeavor" (p. 117). Though it is liable to misunderstanding, authenticity is not an overblown or outdated idea.

Authenticity is Da-sein's appropriation into and of the primal character of its ek-isting, an understanding, Heidegger says, "arising out of one's own Self as such" (1962, p. 186). It assumes freedom. Becoming authentic, as a matter of inner disposition, and acting authentically, as a matter of manifest practice, presupposes essential latitude. What is this leeway? Heidegger's answer, expressed in a deceptively simple manner, is openness. We must take great pains, as he does, not to misinterpret leeway as mere subjective will. Da-sein ek-sists—"stands out" as being t/here—only by virtue of the allowance that the broader reality of being affords. We ek-sist in the openness of being, or, to use another type of speaking, our appearance within or as the openness of being is a configuration of figure and ground. Heidegger exercises many turns of speech to articulate this primordial phenomenon, though we need not trouble ourselves with an enumeration. (We should note, though, that some have not found illuminating or helpful his talk about fields, wood paths, and the like.) We should be able to proceed by means of a flexible handful of cognate notions: openness (perhaps the fundamental term), clearing, room or space, and context or context of emergence. Authenticity is the appropriation or "making one's own" of the essential possibilities of sojourning, which are ill absorbed when left to Da-sein as they-self. It is a recollection of one's own being. Cohn avers:

> [T]herapy could bring about two things: it could enable us to accept the inevitable characteristics of existence—like our being in the body, being with others, the necessity of choice, the certainty of death. But it could also help us to affirm the possibility of choosing our own specific responses to what is "given" (1997, p. 125).

Da-sein's ek-sistence is a balance—or an imbalance, in the case of the constriction or distortion of possibilities—of the factical and the responsive. Da-sein chooses its own(most) way of being in the world into which it is delivered.

"Making one's own," however, does not signify an egoistical act of will, despite the obviously and irreducibly personal nature of existential movement. Da-sein's appropriation of essential possibilities can occur only because Da-sein is appropriated into the clearing that being grants. We may claim possibilities as our own, but in turn we are claimed by the openness of being, which bestows the possibility of making our sojourning truly our own. Thus, as Heidegger says in discussing "The Character of Conscience as a Call": "The call comes *from* me and yet *from beyond me and over me*" (1962, p. 317, p. 320). (Those who are familiar with the novel and film *Fight Club* will recognize this uncanny ontological reflexivity.) Conscience calls us into making the essential possibilities of sojourning our own by reminding us that only we, as thoughtful beings, can take hold of the shape and import of our lives. Peter Wilberg says in *The Therapist as Listener: Martin Heidegger and the Missing Dimension of Counselling and Psychotherapy Training*: "To be a 'client' is to 'be called' in this way—to be on the way to finding oneself as someone who has failed to hear oneself" (2004, p. 22). This avowal may seem to be a truism—realizing, to use the language of *Being and Time*, "something of its {{Da-sein's}} own" (1962, p. 68)—but it is crucially generative for Heidegger inasmuch as he is a hermeneutic philosophical thinker who meditates upon what is closest to us. Van Deurzen says in "Heidegger's Challenge of Authenticity": "Even though we are always ourselves and nobody else we can be ourselves in a non-consuming, inauthentic manner. We have to assume ourselves in order to win our true ownership over our mineness" (1999, p. 116). Monia Brizzi says in "Heidegger and Joy" that "[o]wned [e]xistentiality appears to rise in the leap of freedom of the individual Dasein which opens to and endures the projection and recoiling of the possibility of appropriating its throwness and finitude" (2005, p. 366).

Inauthenticity is a straying from what is closest to us, an occultation of Da-sein's "own Self as such." It is as much a part of Da-sein's way of being as the possibility of authenticity. Heidegger says in *Being and Time*:

> Understanding is either authentic, arising out of one's own Self as such, or inauthentic. The 'in-' of inauthentic does not mean that Dasein cuts itself off from its Self and understands 'only' the world. The world belongs to Being-one's-Self as Being-in-the-world. . . . When one is diverted into . . . one of these basic possibilities of understanding, the other is not laid aside. *Because understanding, in every case, pertains rather to Dasein's full disclosedness as Being-in-the-world, this diversion of the understanding is an existential modification of projection as a whole* (1962, p. 186).

This passage requires some unpacking. Heidegger explains: "As factical {{concretely existing}} Dasein, any Dasein has already diverted its potentiality-for-Being into a possibility of understanding" (p. 186). Da-sein must always exist in this manner or that fashion, in its own way, but in being what it is Da-sein does not necessarily grasp fully its irreducible "ownness." The being of the human being is *"in each case mine"* (p. 67). When Dasein loses its sense of mineness or ownmost decisiveness in the midst of the factical, it exists inauthentically. Cohn says: "Inauthenticity is our denial of the 'given' as well as our denial of the freedom to meet it" (1997, p. 126). While a falling, this losing of mineness or fitting appropriation is not a descent from a pristine state of being; it is not a fall from onto-theological grace. Cohn elaborates that Heidegger

> refuses to see its {{authenticity's}} absence either, theologically, as a state of sin, or, medically, as a state of illness. "Authenticity", the facing of Being as it is, is one of the existential dimensions to which we respond one way or another (1992, p. 92).

The possibility of losing mineness and the possibility of recovering mineness are equiprimordial. Da-sein exists neither in a plenum nor in a void. "Pure" authenticity and inauthenticity are incoherent notions. Pure authenticity as an ideal would require perfect decisiveness and appropriation at every moment, an all-encompassing and unending radiance of clarity, self-possession, and deep movement. This is not Da-sein's reality. We just do find ourselves absorbed into . . . . Pure inauthenticity would mean the absolute impossibility of mineness, yet even in drifting away from mineness Da-sein ek-sists precisely as a *deciding* being whose *ownmost* possibilities recede, as Heidegger says: "So Dasein makes no choices, gets carried along by the nobody, and thus ensnares itself in inauthenticity" (1962, p. 312).

Mills says in "The False Dasein: From Heidegger to Sartre and Psychoanalysis":

> Is there such a clear-cut demarcation between authenticity and inauthenticity? I think not. Instead of these antipodes, we need to understand selfhood as a development on a continuum of authenticity, in a state of becoming as emerging freedom (1997, p. 61).

Authenticity is a modification of the they-self, which is Da-sein's everyday way of being in the world, not an aberration, as Heidegger explains in *Being and Time*:

> For the most part *I myself* am not the "who" of Dasein; the they-self is its "who". Authentic Being-one's-Self takes the definite form of an existentiell modification of the "they"; and this modification must be defined existentially. . . . The "they" has always kept Dasein from taking hold of these possibilities of Being. The "they" even hides the manner in which it has tacitly relieved Dasein of the burden of explicitly *choosing* these possibilities (1962, p. 312).

Inauthenticity as the attenuation of ownmost choice through absorption into . . . is what Da-sein is "for the most part." Brizzi says that "so deeply engulfed in the sedated perversion of average everydayness is inauthentic Dasein that it does not even have any awareness of being entangled and lost in inertia" (2005, pp. 357–358). She adds: "It is . . . intriguing to see how disowning, that which is possible only on the basis of a more primordial owning, seems to be the default position of Dasein" (p. 364). Mills opines:

> In conclusion, I believe there is, for Dasein, a *double edge* of *centeredness*: namely, the authentic center of selfhood is one in the same, inseparable and modally undifferentiated, in that authenticity and inauthenticity exist in symbiosis as the *core dialectical status* of Dasein's Being. Dasein is beyond the authentic and the impure; a disclosure of such unification is its wholeness (1997, p. 61; final set of emphases added).

Cohn warns us, accordingly, that "'authentic' and 'inauthentic' {{should}} not become yet another measure of psychological 'wholeness'" through which a technocratic understanding of the human being takes hold (1997, p. 127). Heidegger says in the *Seminars*:

> Da-sein means being absorbed in that toward which I comport myself, being absorbed in the relationship to what is present, and being absorbed

in what concerns me just now. [It is] a letting oneself be engaged with [*sich-einlassen*] what concerns me (2001, p. 161).

Van Deurzen says plainly and compellingly: "When working with people it is important to remember that they are just as much themselves when they are fallen" (1999, p. 123). The still call of conscience ushers Da-sein into the vicinity of its ownmost possibilities. Thompson says:

> [A]ll human creatures are inauthentic in their nature, but sometimes behave authentically when they rise to the occasion. Of course, we are challenged to do so virtually every moment of our lives, but are usually to distracted to notice (2004, p. 184).

Hall claims strongly, and controversially from the ordinary perspective:

> There is no route from inauthenticity to authenticity that can be planned in inauthenticity. To assume so demonstrates a failure to grasp the distinction between the ontic and the ontological. Indeed, the very notion of goals in therapy, from an ontological perspective, is to limit the possibilities for disclosure to occur in the encounter as they are conceived upon reified and obsolete assumptions in relation to Being-in-the-world (2004, p. 114).

Brizzi argues that Heidegger's lack of examples of authenticity is consistent with the nature of openness, referring to the "impossibility of defining the indefiniteness of Dasein in definite terms that could condemn existence to readiness-to-hand/presence-at-hand and render it obsolete . . ." (2005, p. 362). Mills says in "The False Dasein":

> One is left with a sense of generic ambiguity. Authenticity is opaque and equivocal. It follows a voice that does not speak, it points to a direction that is not visible, it summons us to respond to a calling we cannot identify; yet it appeals to an obligation that cannot be disowned. Perhaps authenticity is *beyond* what words can define; only Dasein knows its truth (1997, pp. 60–61).

The call of conscience, as we will see shortly, "discourses" in the mode of silence: It calls to Da-sein not as a shriek but as a barely audible whisper (even in the fright of anxiety, the true meaning of which Da-sein tends to resist). Da-sein's attunement must be well attuned indeed to attend to this intimation in the midst of the din. Van Deurzen says in *Everyday Mysteries: Existential Dimensions of Psychotherapy*:

Psychotherapists busy themselves attempting to cure people of their anxiety so as to reinsert them into a desacralised world. One wonders if they should not instead be allowing people to experience the call of conscience that makes them anxious and leads to explorations of life that can entrance and fascinate even though this experience may often be rather uncomfortable. How can we cure ourselves of life, when life and its everyday mysteries is all that we have got? (1997, p. 3).

The call of conscience brings us back to life, to a sense of the fullness of possibility.

Heidegger speaks in *Being and Time* of Da-sein's "*Being-guilty*" as "a *kind of Being which belongs to Dasein*" (1962, p. 328). He takes care to distinguish Da-sein's primal Being-guilty from subsequent sorts of guilt such as moral guilt: "The primordial 'Being-guilty' cannot be defined by morality, since morality already presupposes it for itself" (p. 332). "Mistakes" and the like also fall into the category of consequent phenomena (p. 334). Being-guilty is originative—"*indebtedness becomes possible only 'on the basis' of a primordial Being-guilty*" (p. 329). Ordinary, non-originative conceptions of guilt may even compromise Dasein's appreciation of its being-guilty, as calculating shortcomings may turn guilt into a mere technical exercise: "The common sense of the 'they' knows only the satisfying of manipulable rules and public norms and the failure to satisfy them. It reckons up infractions of them and tries to balance them off" (p. 334). In so manipulating and "managing the message," Da-sein as its everyday self leaves aside pharisaically the question of its basic guilt as being t/here. What is this basic guilt? Why is Da-sein guilty in its very being? As a being who chooses possibilities, Da-sein can choose this or that. In choosing *x* over *y*, Da-sein forgoes *y*, and this exclusiveness is an inevitable part of the structure of Da-sein's existence. Da-sein cannot be all things at all times; it can realize its possibilities only one by one, and even then only some of its many possibilities are realizable in a lifetime. Having chosen *x*, Da-sein *is* not-*y*. (Sartre, of course, stresses heavily this pivotal human truth in his theory of consciousness as annihilative.) Heidegger describes this phenomenon as a nullity, for "[f]reedom *is* only in the choice of one possibility—that is, in tolerating one's not having chosen the others and one's not being able to choose them" (p. 331). Wolf explains that guilt as nullity arises

> from my indebtedness because I have a past which must serve as the ground for my existence but over which I have no control, and from my responsibility because on the ground of this past I project particular possibilities and not others (1999, p. 55).

Freedom *is* only through the "not." The "not" grants the meaning of freedom's sway, as Heidegger elaborates:

> Thus "care"—Dasein's Being—means, as thrown projection {{as a situated chooser}}, Being-the-basis of a nullity (and this means Being-the-basis is itself null). This means that *Dasein as such is guilty*, ... Existential nullity has by no means the character of a privation, where something is lacking in comparison with an ideal which has been set up but does not get attained in Dasein; ... This nullity, ... is ... not something which emerges in Dasein only occasionally, attaching itself to it as an obscure quality which Dasein might eliminate if it made sufficient progress (1962, p. 331).

No "progress" can relieve Da-sein of its being-guilty in the face of the nullity that it is. For his own reasons, Kierkegaard would agree with Heidegger's sentiment:

> When Christianity entered into the world, there were no professors or assistant professors at all. It can be assumed that in the present generation every tenth person is an assistant professor; consequently it is a paradox for only nine out of ten. And when the fullness of time finally comes, that matchless future, when a generation of assistant professors, male and female, will live on the earth—then Christianity will have ceased to be a paradox (1992, pp. 220–221).

Da-sein can never experience a "matchless future" in which the "not" of freedom no longer holds sway. We face, as Brizzi says remarkably, "our certain yet indefinite ownmost not-yet" (2005, p. 358). Da-sein's fallenness and its exposure as being t/here are of a piece: "Dasein may ... seek repair and comfort in the tempting ordinary undifferentiatedness of everyday circumspective concern in order to evade its naked uncanniness" (p. 358). To ek-sist means to be in the freedom of the open. Being in the freedom of the open is no guarantee of "success" in any contrived sense or of the "content" of life; as van Deurzen says, "the aim is to achieve careful rather than careless living" (1999, p. 124). Brizzi speculates:

> That in the face of which/about which Dasein flees is selfsame as that in the face of which/about which anxious Dasein is intrigued and that in the face of which/about which calling-hearing Dasein rejoices. It seems that the more existence approximates its own nullity, the less afraid and the more resolute it is! (2005, p. 361).

Sheehan says: "Our lack-in-being 'causes' and maintains our openedness. ... our finitude is the absence that opens the open" (2001, p. 199).

Louis A. Sass explores in "Heidegger, Schizophrenia and the Ontological" the intriguing idea that schizophrenics "might be especially in touch with, or have a heightened awareness of, Being or the ontological difference" (1992, p. 123). He notes that *Being and Time* emphasizes the phenomenon of anxiety as a structural feature of Da-sein's existence: a "cosmic anxiety" in the face of being-in-the-world as such (p. 123). Anxiety is thus an event that discloses Da-sein's status as an enworlded being. Schizophrenics may experience a similar phenomenon in their erstwhile "otherworldly" episodes. Sass speculates that we would do well to consider the odd experiences of schizophrenics not as erroneous digressions from the "real" world—as epistemic mistakes of a sort, as "poor reality-testing"—but as "a domain to which neither belief nor disbelief of the usual kind is of any relevance" (p. 113, p. 115). He argues, for instance, in discussing cases in which schizophrenics feel their experiences happening as though through a camera:

> [S]uch delusional phenomena function as something like symbols for subjectivity itself, for the self-as-subject, and thus they are not objects with*in* the world, whether real or delusional, so much as expressions of the felt ongoing process of knowing or experiencing by *which* this world is constituted (p. 116).

The baroque character of such experiences—how can one "be" a camera (as in one case) or live "through" a camera lens?—does not mean that they are unintelligible, Sass suggests: "Like Being as understood by Heidegger, such phenomena are difficult to locate because they veil themselves precisely by the sheer pervasiveness of their presence" (p. 116). Schizophrenics may be closer to the ontological than a "normal" person, and their peculiar experiences and articulations may result from an "infection of the ontological by the ontic," such that the ontological truth of Da-sein as receiving-perceiving being-in-the-world issues in the person's "becoming a camera" and so on (p. 120). Do these "experiences of a highly general or totalistic nature" count as Heideggerian insights and instances of authentic existence (p. 126)? Sass lists appreciable similarities, though he also states that schizophrenic experiences may illustrate "several variants of subjectivism and objectivism {{metaphysical distortions}} that derive from a forgetting of the true nature of Being and of the difference {{between the ontological and the ontic}}" (p. 126). In short, schizophrenic experience does not fulfill completely the demands of Heideggerian post-metaphysical thinking, but we can gain understanding of such experience—such a way of Da-seining—by employing Heideggerian ideas about the ontological, the ontic, human being, and world.

Psychosis involves a serious break in a person's basic ability to get along in the world. Sass's conclusion (assuming its correctness) is edifying, since many philosophical ideas about psychotherapy and psychopathology apply to non-psychotic phenomena, especially what the *Diagnostic and Statistical Manual of Mental Disorders* used to call neuroses: maladaptive responses that degrade but do not fracture the person's life as a whole. For instance, the philosophical concept of anxiety in *Being and Time*—drawn from Kierkegaard's highly influential existential-religious notion, and taken up in a different form by Sartre—resembles the everyday psychological concept of anxiety. Anxiety disorders (panic attacks and so on), which have been on the rise for years, fell formerly into the category of neurosis. Heideggerian anxiety is a world-disclosing finding, a revealing of everything and thus nothing in particular (unlike fear, which has a discrete referent). In anxiety, the world as world is disclosed; one's being-in-the-world as such becomes apparent; the "nothingness" of freedom (or the "dizziness" of freedom, to use Kierkegaard's turn of phrase) obtrudes. This rising within Da-sein of an awareness of the starkness of being t/here—a disquieting and even arresting sense of "openness"—sounds like a panic attack, in which no thing in particular threatens but in which everything is held open all too plainly. To this extent, Heidegger's insight into the character of anxiety—developed in the 1920s, well before the current rash of anxiety-related problems in living—helps us to understand the (non-psychotic) anxiety disorders. At the same time, his interpretation of anxiety brings to the fore the free yet concrete, enworlded, and relational character of the human being's existing, and all psychological maladies, even the psychoses, are interpretable only through the primal temperament of being t/here. Sass's exploration forces us to try to interpret the "harder case" of psychosis in light of a Heideggerian understanding of the human being, instead of staying only within the sphere of the "easier case" of the "neuroses," as worthwhile and profitable as such may be. If Heidegger's thinking is global in its ramifications, as he hopes it is, we must be able to use it to understand all manner of "psy" phenomena.

3. Openness at the Limit

Openness is not limitless; it is bounded. An open area implies a closed region. We can also invoke Heidegger's notions of unconcealing and concealing: A lighted area implies a surrounding unlighted region. Concealment (Lethe, the river of forgetfulness in the underworld of Greek mythology) accompanies the unconcealing (aletheia, or truth) that grants Da-sein's enworlded being t/here. Moreover, concealment is itself concealed. Thus, a double concealment exists along with unconcealing. This deep constitutive ambiguity suffuses Da-sein's dwelling, but does not obviate the possibility of truth. We misperceive truth, Heidegger believes, when we construe it as just a point of transparency. Truth, understood broadly—understood as the articulation of being—comprises, we can say, "positive" as well as "privative" phenomena. Those things that appear or emerge and those things that recede form a whole ontological reality. (Recall Heraclitus's aphorism: "Nature loves to hide.") Here lies the meaning of Heidegger's claim, in "On the Essence of Truth," that truth is untruth. He is not thereby a postmodern nihilist who obliterates any meaningful conception of truth, but a questioner who is brave enough to admit the intricacy of a truth that foils lazy optimism and impertinent manipulations. The they-self instantiates this double concealment: It covers over being's essential possibilities while veiling this obliqueness, and holds fast to an indulgently thin understanding of self, others, and world. Da-sein's average everydayness talks idly about curiosities that are rooted in purposefully trivial ambiguities, and so Da-sein can overcome its indolence only by abandoning the confused enthusiasms of theyness in favor of reflective reticence. Respect for the thought-provoking truth of being in the world demands a separation from inessential distractions. Indeed, Heidegger goes so far in *Being and Time* as to sanction silence as the method by which Da-sein can become authentic:

> The call {{of conscience}} dispenses with any kind of utterance. . . . *Conscience discourses solely and constantly in the mode of keeping silent.* In this way it not only loses none of its perceptibility, but forces the Dasein which has been appealed to and summoned, into the reticence of itself (1962, p. 318).

Wolf says: "[C]onscience is silent rather than chattering, it has no content to provoke curiosity, and it offers nothing new to gossip about" (1999, p. 56). Conscience discloses Da-sein as disclosing. Conscience discloses disclosing as such. Wolf goes so far as to argue that conscience is "seen to be that element of the ontological structure of Dasein which {{as the disclosing of disclosing}} makes possible phenomenology as a formal philosophical method" (p. 59). Da-sein's call to conscience seems to come from outside itself because the hypnosis of average everydayness makes vital thoughts sound alien, but in truth the beckoning toward authenticity comes from within Da-sein's own concernful being-in-the-world. Wolf understands conscience not as immediate authenticity but as "wanting-to-have-a-conscience", as "joy simply at the *possibility* of recognizing its {{Da-sein's}} individual potentiality-for-being" (p. 57).

The concept of pro-jection (*Entwurf*) is crucial in *Being and Time*. Da-sein's pro-jective structure is central to Heidegger's effort to trace a way to understand "being" through the human condition. Likewise, the notion of "letting be" or releasement (*Gelassenheit*) is salient in some of Heidegger's writings after *Being and Time*. Releasement obviates mere "subjectivity"; the movement of "releasement toward things" invokes an opening of Da-sein to the expansive reality that is the "groundless ground" of everything.

What, then, is the relation between pro-jection and releasement? We can venture that Heidegger puts increasing weight on the "other" in the midst of Da-sein's existence. This development does not mean, however, that the changes in his thinking are so radical as to efface lines of continuity. (Compare Richardson's noted "Heidegger I—Heidegger II" distinction in his *Heidegger: From Phenomenology to Thought*.) Pro-jection and releasement share crucial elements, notwithstanding the temporal distance. We need to keep in mind the recollective nature of thinking.

The English word projection expresses the same connotation that Heidegger intends by *Entwurf*, namely, pro-jection or throwing forward. Graeme Nicholson, in "Ekstatic Temporality in *Sein und Zeit*", translates *Verstehen* as projection, rather than understanding, because he wishes to make clear that disclosure is itself a thrusting-towards and that consequently Da-sein is characteristically "in-advance-of-self" (1986, p. 212). Understanding as such has a pro-jective character. Da-sein's "essence" lies in its existence: its situational, temporal-historical reality of being in the world in one way rather than another. Heidegger characterizes its appearance in the world as thrownness (*Geworfenheit*). Da-sein chooses pro-jectively, throws forward, this possibility, this way of being in the world, and not others. It chooses not only the meaning of its past and present but most vitally its future. Hence, Da-sein is never a "settled" entity; it is a chronically (chronologically) displaced or decentered being. It is always "on the way to . . . ." (*unterwegs zu*). Thus, Nicholson, in interpreting Da-sein's temporal constitution, speaks of "outposting" and "self-exiting" (p. 22). Da-sein ek-sists—stands out. Da-sein's ek-sistence is a gathering together/pressing forward. No particular projects of any sort can arise except by virtue of pro-jection.

As a questioner, Da-sein stands out as a being whose most fitting truth lies in the ontological, which exceeds the realm of absorption in average concerns. Da-sein's appropriation of—appropriation into—questioning conducts it through the everydayness of human designs into the unhomelike (*unheimlich*)—though this uncanniness is itself basic in Da-sein's dwelling. The call of questioning originates in this attunement of unhomelikeness. Spinelli offers in *Tales of Un-knowing* the ideal of reorienting ourselves to the ingenuousness of our receiving-perceiving:

> [U]n-knowing refers to that attempt to remain as open as possible to whatever presents itself to our . . . experience. As such, it expresses the attempt to treat the seemingly familiar, and that of which we are either aware or informed, as novel, unfixed in meaning, accessible to previously unexamined possibilities (1997, p. 8).

Da-sein is a being who, in the ordinariness of its existence, is immersed in concrete ways of acting within the ambit of its interests. This immersion is inevitable, and not "original sin." Even so, open questioning—questioning of the open—is the pro-jective possibility that makes Da-sein unique among beings. Da-sein, in allowing itself to be claimed by the matter of thinking, understands but exceeds its world of commonplace concerns, and any alleged subjectivistic cast of pro-jection dwindles away.

This brief account of pro-jection demonstrates the primacy that Heidegger accords to Da-sein inasmuch as it is the sole interrogator of being (only Da-sein asks the ontological question). How does the stress in *Being and Time* on Da-sein's structure fit with Heidegger's other developments? After all, his statement in "Discourse on Thinking" that humankind must "will not to will" seems to belie his early phenomenological focus on Da-sein. Hubert L. Dreyfus's elaboration of projection certainly rings of hard-nosed pragmatics:

> My understanding activity is directed toward bringing something about. Coping with the available proceeds by pressing into possibilities. Such coping always has a point. The way my coping is organized by a for-the-sake-of-which Heidegger calls *projection*:... (1991, p. 186).

Furthermore, what of the echoes of Kantian transcendental subjectivity? To be sure, the subject does not disappear utterly from Heidegger's thinking; only the subject as a repository of metaphysical prejudice and willfulness vanishes.

Heidegger's later "meditative" thinking frees itself ever more assiduously from the sway of a philosophical structuring in which objects are represented for the benefit of an egological subject. This structuring is a confrontational ontology in which subject and object face one another in an arena of self-assertion and domination. The reality that representational thinking proffers is reality once removed, reality after it has been denuded of its original mystery (self-concealing concealing) and rendered in terms of a will to power that has absolute control as its aim. As David Michael Levin says in *The Listening Self*, this "instrumental projection" of representational thinking is nothing less than a "'projection' of Being": a way of understanding everything that is (1989, p. 23). Now we must ask: Where is the pro-jective subject of *Being and Time* in Heidegger's later thinking?

Heidegger speaks in his later writings of the need for letting be or releasement to things. To use the turn of language in "What Are Poets For?", Da-sein must allow itself to be open to the Open *(Offenheit)*—to be ventured saltatorially in and by being, which precludes any (normal) sort of act of will on Da-sein's part. Even so, Da-sein is not simply passive. If Da-sein were inert, a recollection of being in its existence could not occur at all. Instead, Da-sein "acts" in the special sense that it refrains, while hearkening, from imposing its egoistic ways on the matter of thinking, and abides scrupulously not only by appearing but also by withdrawing. Sheehan speaks of "pres-ab-sential bivalence" (1981, p. 540). Da-sein partakes thereby in the rifted processive fullness of the unfolding of openness—of being. Da-sein is, in this moment, an open-textured self, not a monad of will. Indeed, the will to power espoused by Nietzsche, "the last metaphysician," particularly when construed as technological enframing *(das Ge-stell)*, is the death of Sheehan's de-hypostasized openness. Charles E. Scott says in "Psychotherapy: Being One and Many":

> We experience wholeness as an alertness that pervades and casts an horizon vis-à-vis all present things. We could call it non-voluntary readiness for experience in the midst of experiences, awareness that pervades opposites, a sense of the limitedness of identity, the mood of finiteness, alertness that goes beyond and beneath all that I reflect and know, a sense of sameness with all the differences of my experience (1978–1979, p. 90).

Heidegger's expression "will not to will" should always be taken to include the proviso: "as it were." Releasement toward things precludes willing in the usual sense.

Letting be is "releasement toward things" (*die Gelassenheit zu den Dingen*) and "openness to the mystery" (*die Offenheit für das Geheimnis*), as Heidegger articulates the matter (1966b, p. 55). This is the work of relinquishing the egological standpoint and being responsive to the sending and withdrawing of being in time, to the "It which gives" (*Es gibt*). Heidegger uses the word *Ereignis* to mean the original "event" or "happening" of "appropriation" as the belonging together of being and time, but this belonging together is not only a granting but also, as Kockelmans says, an "ex-propriation," since the event conceals as well as reveals (1984, p. 72). Thus, *Er-eignis* must be thought with *Ent-eignis*. Being and time are appropriated to one another inasmuch as, in belonging together, they are most properly themselves. Nonetheless, though being t/here *is* time-ly caring, the truth of being/time recedes from the purview of Da-sein. This ebb exposes the scantiness of representational thinking and merely propositional statements—in short, any reifying orientation. Compare the opening passages of Lao Tzu's *Tao Te Ching*:

> In perennial nonbeing you see mystery,
> and in perennial being you see appearance.
> Though the two are one and the same,
> once they arise, they differ in name.
> One and the same, they're called *dark-enigma*,
> dark-enigma deep within dark enigma,
> gateway of all mystery (2000, p. 3).

To speak in the language of "On the Essence of Truth", we should think concealment (*lethe*) as the heart of unconcealment or truth (*aletheia*), as the privative "a-" suggests. The unfolding of being and time is not amenable to being inspected and rendered translucent. *Ereignis* invokes the withering away of self-assertion. The necessity for Da-sein to "will not to will" remains. Da-sein is, questioningly and uncannily, brought to the source of its dwelling. How different, though, is Da-sein the ontological questioner as enunciated in *Being and Time*?

Da-sein the projective being of *Being and Time* is not only thrown into the world (*Geworfenheit*): It throws forward possibilities *(Entwurf)*, even with respect to its past (it gives meaning to its past). The possibility of taking up the matter of thinking lies among its choices. Upon adopting this possibility, however, Da-sein leaves behind its familiar habitat in favor of "what gives us food for thought before all else and always", as Heidegger says in *What is Called Thinking?* (1968, p. 45). It heeds the call of conscience, which discourses in the mode of silence, inaudible to those who are acclimatized to the din of the ontic. Heidegger states in *Being and Time*:

> The call discourses in the uncanny mode of *keeping silent*. And it does this only because, in calling the one to whom the appeal is made, it does not call him into the public idle talk of the "they", but *calls* him *back* from this *into the reticence of his existent* potentiality-for-Being (1962, p. 322).

While he is here emphasizing Da-sein's concern for itself, he also says: "The call comes *from* me and yet *from beyond me*" (p. 320). Compare this statement from the early 1950's: "*Language speaks as the peal of stillness.* . . . The peal of stillness is not anything human" (1971, p. 207).

The emphasis in *Being and Time* on existential analytic is transfigured into an inflection on the trans-subjective and indeed trans-human dimension of our life. Michael Gelven, in discussing the projective nature of *Verstehen,* confirms that "[a]lthough such {{projective}} existence is mine [*eigen*], it is always more than what I am" (1984, p. 186). As Heidegger has one of the figures in "Conversation on a Country Path about Thinking" say approvingly: "You want a non-willing in the sense of a renouncing of willing, so that through this we may release, or at least prepare to release, ourselves to the sought-for essence of a thinking that is not a willing" (1966a, pp. 59–60). David Wood explains:

> Heidegger has always avoided the hint of subjective activity that the term "*constitution*" might be thought to imply. . . . So time cannot be something we add to raw data to create temporally complex objects. Rather, through the opening, the time-space, as he comes to call it, Being gives itself, or *it gives (es gibt),* or there is an *event of appropriation* (*ereignis*) (1989, p. 253).

John Sallis says in discussing understanding:

> [T]he determination of understanding as projection brings more fully into relief a certain decentered or disoriented character that, *all along*, differentiates it from positing (*Setzen*) in the transcendental sense. . . . Dasein cannot but project upon a possibility that both is most proper to itself and yet absolutely cannot be appropriated (1990, p. 143; emphasis added).

Pro-jection—"leaping" within/to being—is not, as George Kovacs points out, a notion born of a "philosophy of subjectivity" (1992, pp. 48–49). Instead, it is a leaping that takes place strictly by virtue of being itself. The leap (*der Sprung*) to or for being is a leap *by* being. Being is itself pro-jective in this originative (*ursprünglich*) sense. As Heidegger says in *Contributions to Philosophy (From Enowning)*: "[The leap] is the enactment of projecting-open the truth of be-ing in the sense of shifting into the open, such that the thrower of the projecting-open experiences itself as thrown—i.e., as en-owned by be-ing" (1999, p. 169).

The *Verstehen* that Nicholson translates as pro-jection rather than understanding is constitutive of Da-sein as a temporal-historical being, an enworlded being who exists in rich particularity. *Verstehen* in the matter of thinking is letting be or releasement. Being "in-advance-of-self" here means being "outside-of-self" (ek-static dwelling): an understanding of self and world that acknowledges the uncanny "It which gives." Gerald L. Bruns, in thinking through Heidegger's decisive enunciation of the estranging effect of poetry, goes so far as to liken the call (which is "uncanny discourse") with madness:

> It means belonging to a place where everything is other than usual, where the *gewöhnlich* {{normal or ordinary}} has been displaced but not replaced by anything determinate that, given time, we could become familiar with—not replaced, in short, by something new or advanced (1989, p. 72).

Of course, this uncanniness is no objection to Heidegger's articulation of the matter; "displaced but not replaced" simply tells us how the matter stands with Da-sein as being t/here. Replacement is an idea that smacks of absorption in insular plans; "displacement" voices the reality of the questioning, thoughtful Da-sein traversing the a/lethic region of *Ereignis*. *Being and Time*'s Da-sein is radicalized—gathered to its root—as questioner. The manner in which we "belong" in everyday engrossment is not the manner in which we "belong" (*gehören*) in ontological self-exiting, in which we hear (*hören*) the call of *Ereignis*, in which we heed the intimation that being t/here as time-ly caring in the allowance which being gives must come into "its" own (*Eignen*). Thus, Parvis Emad speaks fittingly of the "appropriat*ing* throw of being and appropriat*ed* throw of Dasein" (1991, p. 32). Pro-jection (*Entwurf*) and thrownness (*Geworfenheit*) coalesce uniquely in Heidegger's saying of *Ereignis*. Sheehan says:

> What Heidegger is expressing in both the earlier language of *Geworfenheit* and the later language of *Ereignis* is that being-open is the ineluctable condition of our essence, not an occasional accomplishment of our wills. It is our "fate," the way we already are (2001, p. 194).

He largely resists the common translation of *Ereignis* as appropriation, instead arguing in favor of "bringing something out into view," while allowing that the word appropriation "might work—but only if we understand the *proprium* of appropriation as the opening up of openness" (p. 196, p. 198). In the end, Sheehan contends, Heidegger's topic is "our finitude as opening up the world/clearing/open that we essentially are"; "[o]ur finitude is the 'it' that 'gives being' . . . [o]ur finitude is *die Sache selbst* {{the matter itself}}" (p. 200, p. 199).

Heidegger interjects near the end of the "Conversation" a one-word fragment of Heraclitus: "Αγχιβασίη" (*anchibasie*), which Kathleen Freeman translates as "approximation" (1983, p. 33). His initial rendering is "going toward," though a short while later he weighs "going near" (1966a, p. 88, p. 89). Heidegger rests finally with "moving-into-nearness" or, even more faithfully to *Ereignis*, "letting-oneself-into-nearness" (p. 89). This movement in the text is a re-sounding of the movement from the pro-jection of *Being and Time* to the letting be or releasement of his later thinking, a development in which, nevertheless, we see the constant element of drawing near (*nahe*), of "neighboring" with being or being in nearness (*die Nähe*) with it. As Frank Schalow articulates the matter, we see the "offering of an openness *(der Offenheit),* which propels the self into the ecstatic disclosedness of the 'there'" (1992, p. 80). This radical gathering together of Da-sein and (its) being, while a drawing near, embodies the primordial and inexhaustible truth of ontological opacity. Heidegger exhorts us at the climax of "Memorial Address" to "releasement toward things and openness to the mystery" (1966b, p. 55). His conjunction here is no accident. The uncanny (*unheimlich*) character of the "bracketing" of the mundane grants us awareness of the mystery (*Geheimnis*).

Heidegger states in *Identity and Difference*: "Man *is* essentially this relationship of responding to Being, this relation of co-responding, and he is only this. This 'only' does not mean a limitation, but rather an excess" (2002, p. 31). This "excess" is nothing less than the ek-static—pro-jective/opening—reality of Da-sein. This ek-static truth "grant[s] us the possibility of dwelling in the world in a totally different way" (1966b, p. 55).

Four

FURTHER CONNECTIONS

Heidegger's influence on psychology has been much more limited than his effect on philosophy. Nonetheless, his thinking has helped to shape two philosophically inspired streams within psychology, phenomenology and existentialism, and has generated an explicitly Heideggerian psychological approach, Daseinsanalysis. Regarding phenomenological paths, we may concentrate profitably on Spinelli's emphasis on the "being qualities" of the participants in psychotherapy (an emphasis that is also existential) and Gendlin's use of focusing, which, as already discussed, guides us into the process of emergence. Regarding existentialism, Sartre's forbidding and combative metaphysical psychology is an obvious standard of reference, though van Deurzen, a contemporary figure, captures better the air of Heidegger's thinking about psychology with the title of her book *Everyday Mysteries*. Heidegger's work also bears upon humanistic psychology, at least to the extent that humanistic psychologists appeal to Heideggerian ideas. Finally, Daseinsanalysis as developed by Boss offers itself as a kind of psychoanalysis (Boss was a psychiatrist and a psychoanalyst), so the question of the relation between a Heidegger-inspired psychology and psychoanalysis demands our attention. Heidegger's approach at all times places at a distance physicalistic and reductionistic ways of understanding and treating human beings. It opposes any slant or method that disallows or diminishes our being t/here.

1. Experience and Meaning

Heidegger's explicit remarks about psychology and the general implications of his thinking bear some similarity to, and have a bearing upon, Gestalt approaches to psychology. Such approaches emphasize phenomenological awareness and process, openness to experience, the discovery of meaning, and psychosomatic integration. They also usually assume a fundamentally hopeful humanistic orientation. The more florid aspects of the history of Gestalt psychotherapy have nothing in common with Heidegger's perspective. We should focus on the more conservative elements of Gestalt psychology in our effort to make connections.

The German word Gestalt means roughly configuration. The configuration or structure of a phenomenon comprises the figure or foreground and the ground or background. For example, at this moment these words are figure or foreground, while the remainder of the page is ground or background—part of current experience, naturally, but not as saliently as these words right here and now. The ground or background includes many other items and qualities on different levels, such as the sensation of holding the back of the book, the unseen portion of the room or space, and the rationale for reading this book in the first place. The early psychophysical or perceptual Gestaltists pioneered such investigations, so creating the groundwork for Gestalt psychotherapy. For Gestalt psychotherapists, then, perception and experience always involve structure of this sort, a configurative play between what appears or moves into awareness and what recedes. What is figure can withdraw into ground, and what is ground can emerge as figure. Some Gestaltists extend background as far as transpersonal sources of experience. Gestaltists prefer to conceive ground as that which is not figure at the moment but could be so in principle, rather than unconscious material in a strong sense. Thus, Gestalt as a general psychological perspective is optimistic (as it must be if it is humanistic): Autonomy lies within reach.

Our perception and experience are marked inevitably by the rhythms of the relative or temporary inaccessibility of some aspects of the totality of our world, but as organisms we seek completion and integrity (or, to use a Gestalt term that popular culture has adopted, "closure"). We achieve a "good Gestalt" or locus of meaning when we become aware concretely of resolvent play between figure and ground. Good Gestalts are likely to arise when we are open to experience in its fullness. While the lived flow of our organismic existence is a complex set of processes that includes conditions of an occlusive nature, we have a drive and an innate ability to appropriate "lost" features of our whole truth as human beings. The ripeness of experience includes all manner of bodily, affective, and creative realities, not just the intellect. The intellect is a fundamental part of human organisms, but one who lives merely intellectually "lives in his head." As Petruska Clarkson says in *Gestalt Counselling in Action*: "Gestalt is an approach which emphasises right-hemispheric, non-linear thinking—not at the expense of other ways of knowing but as a complement to these" (2004, p. 2).

The similarities to Heidegger are clear enough. He ponders at the greatest length appearing, withdrawing, and concealing as primal cadences of unfolding. Heidegger leaves aside "consciousness" in any modernist or transcendental sense—a Cartesian and Husserlian preoccupation—and prefers faithful phenomenological discourse about what appears as it appears. He calls for openness to human being, earth, and cosmos, an original experiencing of unfolding such as it is. Meaning lies in Da-sein's encounter with self, other, things, and ultimately "that which gives." In short, Heidegger aspires to a deep and integrated understanding of humanity, things, and universe.

Gestalt as a psychotherapeutic practice takes typically an unabashedly humanistic slant, thus distancing itself from the numinous quality of Heideggerian thinking. Da-sein is responsible for its existence—as the Gestalt client is "response-able" for herself—but Heidegger does not presuppose "humanism" or "autonomy" (or hence optimism) in the standard senses. Instead, his Da-sein is a being who is free to the extent that "what gives" allows Da-sein into the purview of thinking. Da-sein chooses and acts, but only by virtue of being t/here. While a unique prospect of unfolding, the human being is not the touchstone of the Heideggerian cosmos. Da-sein is an ontologically interrogative prospect. Meaning originates with Da-sein as ek-static being t/here, not the human being as a "self-determining organism." The ideal of an organism that wills betrays ontological myopia and hubris. However much Da-sein desires and plans and pro-jects itself into the future, being t/here's most primitive experience is the self-concealing truth of its uncanny emergence into and being-held-in ek-sistence. The uncanniness is irresolvable, and ought to engender recognition of participation in a broader movement that exceeds totalization. Though a questioner, Da-sein cannot turn itself into a metaphysical Panopticon. Thinking concedes its meagerness. Humility is the appropriate response to this most primitive experience. Da-sein lives locally, but may not sensibly indulge egoism or mere subjectivity. Whatever concrete pursuits Da-sein enjoys, Da-sein's enworldedness is a granting, not an entitlement. On a Heideggerian view, the organism of Gestalt, perhaps save transpersonal interpretations, might smack of self-importance. Organic physicality, for instance, is a reality that, while customized, Da-sein shares with all other forms of life. We must beware of construing Da-sein's directionality and rhythms as founded on an egoistically preoccupied self. The play of being t/here's ek-sistence is the play of being itself. All told, approaches to Gestalt vary, and enough similarities to Heidegger's thinking exist to warrant further investigation and efforts at bridging.

Victor Frankl's logotherapy distinguishes somatic, psychic, and noetic levels in the human being. The somatic dimension is the obvious bodily reality of existence. The psychic dimension is the mental and psychological apparatus of the person. The noetic dimension is the uniquely human meta-somatic and meta-psychic zone in which s/he strives for and grasps meaning. While rationality enjoys pride of place in Aristotle's analysis of the human being (the other levels are the vegetative and the animal), here the inimitably human element is the life of meaning. The life of meaning does not preclude or exclude rationality, but rationality is a narrower category than meaning. A "rational" life void of meaning would be humanly unrecognizable. A body and mind do not by themselves constitute a practicable human existence; a "will to meaning" must make itself felt for the human being as a whole to persist and flourish. Frankl's own experiences in Nazi death camps attest to this existential truth. Some prisoners with (under the circumstances) sufficiently sound bodies and minds either succumbed surprisingly quickly or attempted suicide. We must include in the category of the psychic the panoply of psychological phenomena, and depression materialized frequently and quickly in new inmates. Frankl asks whether, in the typical case, the depression created a sense of meaninglessness or futility or whether a perceived lack of meaning engendered the clinical depression. He speculates that "noölogical" failure—an inability to see and stick to meaning—explains many such cases. Nietzsche's famous aphorism is highly apposite: "If we have our own *why* of life, we shall get along with almost any *how*" (1982b, p. 468). Frankl insists on the truth of this idea, regarding himself and his fellow prison camp inmates as examples of meaning-until-the-very-moment-of-death: the thoroughgoing suffusion of our existence with the noölogical. A person, he says, is always free to heed the call of meaning, even in fatal circumstances. The call to meaning spans the mundane and the momentous.

Frankl views the human being as reflexive, and thus as unlike the animal. Human beings are able to stand back and regard themselves, so human beings are beings of existential distance: They open and double back. Reflection affords a person a chance to respond differently. Frankl considers humor to be a phenomenon of distance: Laughing is release through detachment. He says:

> [H]umor helps man rise above his own predicament by allowing him to look at himself in a more detached way. So humor would also have to be located in the noetic dimension. After all, no animal is able to laugh, least of all at himself (1967, p. 4).

We are beings who, in standing in the world, stand back as well, which is a kind of incongruity; therefore, we are (must be!) humorous. According to Frankl, our ability to detach ourselves from the immediate also explains the (alleged) efficacy of the distinctively logotherapeutic technique of paradoxical intention. Paradoxical intention involves asking a person to try hard to commit the very action that she wishes to avoid (for example, stuttering). (Boss's simple challenge "Why not?" also comes to mind.) Frankl claims that in many cases the incongruity of this situational demand renders the person unable to perform the undesirable behavior, and, furthermore, that logotherapy alone can account for this effect through its emphasis on the noetic. The issue of whether other approaches can account for the claimed effectiveness of paradoxical intention is an open question.

For Frankl, the *logos* or primal sense or character of human being is the will to meaning, not the will to pleasure (Freud) or the will to power (Nietzsche), which are just offshoots of the will to meaning. (p. 6). Thus, psychological perspectives that latch onto the undeniably real but cruder aspects of our constitution distract us from what we could be by virtue of the extensive richness of our human nature, from our unique calling as beings who are infused with and moved by meanings. Nietzsche, too, emphasizes meaning, but Nietzschean meaning is inescapably humanly determined in a strong sense: No objective meaning whatsoever exists, because no objective stance exists or can exist. Each instance of life—each organism, whether human or non-human—

proceeds by way of its own distinct perspective, so the number of perspectives equals the number of instances of life. An organism cannot break out of its perspective and achieve an impartial, "God's eye" view of reality; it can know reality only through its own lens, and apparent breakthroughs into objectivity are just variations or distensions of local perspective, not the transcendence of perspective altogether. So the meanings by which human beings live are, in the end, organismic values. These values are thoroughly human—or, as Nietzsche argues forcefully, too frequently "human, all too human." His formula is simple: Either values advance life or they hinder it. The individual human being can never discover values—they are not "ready-made things" that await apprehension by human beings, as Beauvoir says in *The Ethics of Ambiguity* (1997, p. 35)—but can only create values. All value is an expression of the biological. The only feature that differentiates significantly human beings from other forms of life is braininess (he says that we are "the clever animals" and that "[t]he intellect, . . . unfolds its chief powers in simulation"), but even this attribute is utterly physical and nothing more than an evolutionary adaptive strategy (whether successful in a particular case or not) (1982a, p. 42, p. 43). This exaltation of the will to power is the logical conclusion of the history of Western metaphysics, Heidegger claims, for reasons that lie beyond the scope of this book. At the other end of the axiological spectrum, Frankl holds that values can never be "merely subjective": Meanings are meaningful only because they have an objective status. (Nietzsche would interpret the insistence on the objectivity of values as just another example of the "need to believe" as a thoroughly perspectival organismic coping tactic.) He does not demonstrate, however, that or how this is the case. Thus, we are left without a clear and compelling sense of the logotherapeutic understanding of meaning—and understanding is the critical word. Being t/here as encountering takes in what is given, and what is given could not be such in the absence of this reception. The hermeneutic circle of interpretation is the originative reality of taking something as . . . in all our dealings. World is not an objective entity "out there"; it is the full manner in which Da-sein moves concernfully. Recognizing Da-sein's complex wholeness as an opening in/of being obviates any need to emphasize the so-called objectivity of meaning.

Behavioral approaches to therapy, though they might be effective in some cases, do not conform to the spirit of Heideggerian philosophy. On a Heideggerian view, such approaches evince an unfortunately reductive and even despotic imperative. The tendency toward "the outer" is a distortion of Da-sein's whole being, but not because "the inner" is more important—any strong distinction between inner and outer collapses because of the power of the holistic concept of being-in-the-world. The technocratic drive to manipulate variables seeks a standardization and (whether understood or not) miniaturization of the human being. It issues in an arid regime of mechanization that quashes the fullness of the unfolding of Da-sein's possibilities. Cognitive approaches to therapy fare better in principle in a Heideggerian context, but problems and concerns of significance remain. The technically achieved alteration of specific beliefs and attitudes as a goal of psychotherapy represents a wish to impose a regime of efficiency on "the inner." For Heidegger, however, no technique can address completely the peculiar nature of the person as primal being t/here. Furthermore, he understands beliefs and so on as possible only on the basis of primitive un/concealing (see "On the Essence of Truth"), so such a preoccupation disregards or takes too lightly more original phenomena.

2. Leaping Ahead with Da-sein

Boss attests that Heidegger

> confided in me that he had hoped that through me—a physician and psychotherapist—his thinking would escape the confines of the philosopher's study and become of benefit to wider circles, in particular to a large number of suffering human beings (1978–1979, p. 7).

Despite initial difficulties, Heidegger and Boss managed to cultivate a rich application of Heidegger's philosophical ideas to psychotherapy known as Daseinsanalysis. While Binswanger coined the term in the thirties, Boss is the figure who is most associated with the development of a truly Heideggerian psychotherapy in the fifties and sixties. He and others founded the first Daseinsanalytic institute in Zürich in the early seventies. Scott says that Binswanger and Boss, both purveyors of their own kind of "talking cure," retained "the practice of psychoanalysis while rejecting Freudian metapsychology" (1990, p. 133). Scott explains that they founded their variation of psychotherapeutic practice

> not . . . {{on the preconception of}} . . . a sick subject but . . . a way of being that *is* world-openness {{receiving-perceiving}} and that can injure itself by types of severe closure to its own openness in its ways of being with people and things (p. 139).

Thus, the goal of therapy is "restoring a non-technical, living attunement to Da-sein's *Seinsverständnis* {{understanding of Being, or Da-sein as understanding being t/here}}" so that "distortions give way to a freer, more open responsiveness to the claims that make up one's being-in-the-world" (p. 140). Richardson says: "As a liberating from darkness (*léthé*), this truth {{of psychotherapy}} is essentially freedom, and freedom of this kind comes to pass through the functioning of language" (2003, p. 98). Hersch conceives psychopathology as a restriction of an individual's range of possibilities, or a significant narrowing of his or her horizons as a whole. The aim of treatment, therefore, would be to free up more of those possibilities, or widen that individual's horizons (p. 186).

Da-sein as receiving/perceiving being t/here always and already understands itself, others, things, and its world. It has the ability to refine, extend, and appropriate more fully this articulation in pro-jecting itself into its future. Even so, Da-sein is never resolute unwaveringly for the duration of its ek-sistence, so it stands to benefit from the well-attuned helping gestures—the anticipatory care—of fellow Da-seins that serve as a cultivating reminder of the call to freedom, responsibility, and authenticity.

One of Boss's signature psychotherapeutic devices is his use of the question "Why not?" as a prod to the client's articulation of her way of being in the world. The Daseinsanalytic use of this seemingly sarcastic but in fact solicitous question is intended to open up possibilities for the client, such that her being-in-the-world is freed for greater clarity, thoughtful appropriation of possibilities, and personal responsibility. In asking "Why not?", Boss concretizes therapeutically what Heidegger calls "anticipatory care": caring that "leaps ahead" both of and with the other to encourage her in living a freer and more responsible existence. This leaping-ahead is distinct from, and superior to, "intervening care," in which one "leaps in for" the other in a way that leaves her relatively dependent and inarticulate (1962, p. 158). "Inarticulate" does not mean, of course, that the other is unable to speak in a superficially or externally adequate manner. Instead, as Heidegger explains, intervening care discourages her movement toward appropriating her ownmost possibilities:

> This kind of solicitude takes over from the Other that with which he is to concern himself. The Other is thus thrown out of his own position; he steps back so that afterwards, when the matter has been attended to, he can either take it over as something finished and at his disposal, or disburden himself of it completely (p. 158).

Such leaping-for diminishes the other's responsiveness to the call of existential appropriation, and yields a "constricted Dasein," as Mills says in "The False Dasein" (1997, p. 46). Indeed, such leaping-for diminishes the therapist, since, according to Boss, the "most fundamental purpose" of psychotherapy is "for the therapist to respond to the appeal of the patient to be" (1988, p. 61). As Gion Condrau explains: "All such prescriptions, . . . whether of medication or advice, have the untherapeutic potential of creating an ultimately demeaning and unhealthy dependency" (1988, p. 120). Heidegger states in *Being and Time* in the section "The Dasein-with of Others and Everyday Being-with":

> [T]here is . . . the possibility of a kind of solicitude which does not so much leap in for the Other as leap ahead of him in his existentiell potentiality-for-Being, not in order to take away his 'care' but rather to give it back to him authentically as such for the first time (1962, pp. 158–159).

Leaping ahead of the other "frees the Other in his freedom for himself" (p. 159). Boss states that "the whole of daseinsanalysis, what Heidegger's teaching has taught me" is "only to open my eyes":

> And also this is the whole direction that phenomenology or daseinsanalysis can give to a patient: to help him to open his eyes and to look at the things themselves and not to build theories beforehand and then to look through the theories to the human being (1988, p. 41).

Daseinsanalytic work, Boss claims, is crucially premised on "your {{the therapist's}} actual being together with your patients in the knowledge of this task of engagement of human be-ing"—"not so much what you know intellectually" (1988, p. 43). So "actual being together" signifies the work of helping the other to articulate his human condition, and thus to dwell in the world in a different way. Otherwise, we will achieve at best a "more polished object," to recall Heidegger's critique of overly technical psychotherapeutic approaches. As he says in the *Seminars*: "[T]he relationship between the one who does the Daseinsanalysis [the analyst] and the one who is analyzed [the analysand] can be experienced as a relationship between one Da-sein and another" (2001, p. 124). Bo Jacobsen in "Is Gift-Giving the Core of Existential Therapy?" quotes Yalom on the nature of existential therapy:

> Both patient and therapist have to confront the same deep existential issues in life. So we are much more equal than not. And the therapist should not hide anything from the patient, but be open. It is not the content; it is the changes in the relationship that defines existential therapy (2003, p. 347).

Thus, Richardson states:

> For the primordial experience of truth will appear not in a judgment about what is the case {{as in strong versions of cognitive therapy}}, but what is the case itself in so far as it lets itself be seen (e-vident), that is the way things are in their very self-disclosure (2003, p. 89).

Da-sein is an un/concealing; its ek-sistence is revelatory in the manner of throwing thrownness. Da-sein is, as Boss puts the matter, a "bundle of possible relationships" (1988, p. 44). As a bundle of possible relationships, questioning possibilities—ways of being in the world—is incumbent upon Da-sein. (If Da-sein were not a being of possibilities, then it would be simply an object. Stones change, but they have no possibilities.) While these possibilities that Da-sein is are indeed multitudinous, they are limited by Da-sein's death, and so Da-sein is aware of itself as mortal. Da-sein is a mortal who questions itself—its possible ways of being—and in so doing it necessarily questions out of its own experience as dwelling in this place at this time under these environing circumstances with these other human beings. In other words, out of its extant understanding Da-sein further interprets its self, others, things, and world. Articulation in the dictionary sense involves the sense of "joining," and in truth the movement of interpretive questioning opens Da-sein in its being to joinings of possibilities. This utterly processive call is, as Boss says, the "task of engagement of human be-ing." Da-sein is in a position to appropriate its ownmost possibilities only when it is open in a freely responsive manner to the call to be. Heidegger says in the *Seminars* that "[t]o stand under the claim of presence is the greatest claim made upon a human being" (2001, p. 217). Indeed, he continues, "[i]t is 'ethics' [in the original sense]" (p. 217). The Heideggerian cosmos claims us ("ethically"): "We stand before phenomena, which require us to become aware of them and to receive-perceive them in an appropriate manner" (p. 28). Detachment from phenomena is impossible, and the nature of Da-sein's response to the phenomena of its world evinces its condition as a receiving-perceiving opening. As un/concealment, Da-sein can drift heedlessly into absorption into . . . , and thus into forgetting, or it can advert heedfully to its own living condition of shaping at every moment its ek-static sojourning.

Kockelmans says that "psychology and psychiatry already actually exist and . . . *Daseinsanalysis* merely presents them with a critical reflection on their foundations" (1995, p. 539). As a regional ontology, Daseinsanalysis "is not a substitute for psychology and psychoanalysis, nor is it some kind of psychotherapeutic method of practice" (p. 540). What, then, does it have to offer? Kockelmans's statement is worth quoting at length:

> {{It is}} a new methodical approach to human reality. Its function in regard to psychology and psychoanalysis is threefold: 1) to clarify the genuine meaning of the ontological frameworks from which these sciences thematize their respective subject matters; 2) to examine the presuppositions and basic conceptions of both psychology and psychiatry with respect to their adequacy in regard to the fundamental mode of Being of man; 3) to provide psychology and psychoanalysis with new impulses for research and confront them both with problems which until now remained hidden. *Daseinsanalysis* attempts to achieve these goals by foregoing all traditional, theoretical abstractions and constructions in order instead to focus directly on the phenomena themselves which can be experienced immediately (p. 540).

On this view, psychotherapy is a matter of allowing and entering the client's world: of letting it be and letting it show itself as it is. As a "talking cure"—including discoursing in the mode of silence—the client's use of language "point[s] to a certain conception of world in which the speaker lives or has lived, as well as to the way in which this particular type of ex-istence surpasses what is, toward the world, toward Being" (p. 543). As a being of possibilities, Da-sein surpasses or transcends; it ek-sists as understanding projection in its world of concerns. Leaping ahead with Da-sein for the sake of its freedom means letting the client's felt being-in-the-world be in its fullness, as the encounter permits. Any sort of approach to the human being—scientific or otherwise—is founded on the primordial reality of Da-sein as being t/here.

As we have seen, Spinelli's advocacy of being-with and being-for the client as indispensable ingredients of therapy brings to mind Heidegger's injunction to leap-ahead in anticipatory care instead of leaping-for in intervening care. The nomenclatural differences are insignificant. Spinelli's being-with and being-for are equivalent to Heidegger's anticipatory care. Both praxes embody steadfast receptivity to the other's being-in-the-world and persevering willingness to be-with this fellow Da-sein in her quest for the unfolding of meaning. Acknowledging and trying to enter into the client's experience is necessary if the aim of therapy is to enable the client to live out more fully her truth as engaged being-in-the-world. Both praxes forswear the confinement of one's fellow Da-sein in an authoritarian relationship in which the client is unduly dependent or a therapeutic situation that is riddled with theoretical contraptions. The possible danger of theory resides in the distance between concepts and experience, as Spinelli elaborates: "Any theory that we care to formulate (including, of course, phenomenological theory) is the result of reflective experience, since it is an attempt to provide some hierarchy of significance to any straightforward experience" (1989, p. 24). An urge to "treat" or "cure" a client's "symptoms" may belie an impatient and therefore insufficiently attentive and scantily experiential therapeutic orientation. Whatever one's intentions, intervening care blocks the existential requirement for the client as engaged being-in-the-world to appropriate more fittingly her ownmost possibilities. Anticipatory care endeavors to draw out the client's ever-present implicit understanding of her potentiality-for-being, and the key to this drawing out is, to use Spinelli's way of speaking, "being qualities," a reality that Wilberg also addresses in *The Therapist as Listener*. On his view, listening is not just a "communication skill" but a basic part of being-with. Wilberg states:

> Listening as a *relational practice* is a practice of being with others in silence which requires the listener to be both fully 'there' (*Da-sein*) and to be fully *with* the other (*Mit-sein*). Yet being fully *there* and *with* the other requires not just the professional attention or personal empathy of the lis-

tener but their fully embodied presence as a human being (2004, pp. 1–2).

On his account, therapy happens in the "interhuman space" to which both client and therapist "belong" mutually in "hearing together" (p. 13). Wilberg locates listening not in just one person, let alone only in one person's ears, but in both persons as a total situation. He cautions us, as Spinelli does, against a technician's grasp of the total situation: "[L]istening can never be reduced to a set of skills and techniques that we learn in order to 'listen in role'—. . ." (p. 19). The person—the being-in-the-world—of the therapist is vital: "Training in listening 'skills' and 'techniques' implies that it makes no difference *who* is listening as long as the 'how' {{of?}} listening is got right away—conforming to the professional specifications of the role" (p. 19). Wilberg even questions the worth of standard psychotherapeutic techniques such as repeating the client's words for clarity: "Only by listening to and addressing a client with one's whole being—by silently 'sounding someone out' and not merely echoing or addressing them verbally—are they really 'called', addressed in their very being" (p. 21). Susanna Rennie says in "Fever or Forgotten Wings: The Relevance of Heidegger's Call of Conscience to Psychotherapy":

> In the stillness of therapy known as "holding" {{patient attending}}, the client may feel able to open up to their own experience. However, the silence that Heidegger speaks of is invariably difficult for both client and trainee therapist, because it interrupts the listening away {{distracted attention}} that keeps us at a safe distance (2001, p. 279).

Heidegger's novel uses of language summon the reader or listener "out of complacency—from the worn-out familiarity with words, where original meanings have been concealed—and challenges us to actively reflect on what he is trying to communicate and how we experience it" (p. 281). In the end, she argues, we should focus on pursuing concretely the "*way in*" that Heidegger offers, not on spinning out even more recherché glosses of his writings (p. 269). The "way in" here means palpating the saturant reality of our own being-in-the-world. All else follows from this mindfulness. This lucid observance of being-in-the-world as being t/here in its manifold "modes" promises a more apposite self-understanding. The lucid observance can only be, however, a heedfully lived series of chosen and re-chosen processes—but it can never be (somehow) a dead *fait accompli* within Heidegger's writings. Wolf in "Heidegger's Conscience" says for a similar purpose: "Heidegger's text is not claiming authenticity, but a readiness for the possibility of being called by conscience to authenticity" (1999, p. 60).

CONCLUSION

We have negotiated primary themes of Heidegger's thinking as they inform matters of psychology. We must now gather these conceptions and affinities into a summary account of what propitious "psy" endeavors might look like from a Heideggerian perspective. While Daseinsanalysis as developed by Boss is the most prominent (and the official) direct psychological descendant of Heidegger's philosophy, the implications of his thinking are broad and can shape many other complementary approaches and applications.

We see plainly that Heidegger rejects any orientation, explicitly scientific or otherwise, that construes the human being as an object or thing-like entity. We ought not to approach human beings as physical "units" that are amenable to dissection—though they are biological, and, as biological, are obviously analyzable and manipulable physically. To be a human being is to be in the world in a manifestly physical way, but the lived physicality of the human being is not simply the gross actuality of the body. To believe so is to mistake the fundamental condition of the human being. Embodiment is bodying forth, which is a broad interpretive and directional human reality. Beyond the immediate issue of the body, we see that Heidegger eschews any perspective that reduces the human being in the fullness of her being to a "case" to be "managed." The human being is indeed intelligible—always and already interpretable—but is "manageable" only at a great hermeneutic cost. Manageability implies manipulability, which implies in turn simplification and control. Heidegger salvages the uniqueness of human being from vantages that distort and denude its ontological panoply. While granting, as we must, the vast and imposing reality of physicality and all object-ively determining conditions, we need to allow into our thinking the prospect of our human opening as a "noetic edge" in being, an interrogative opening without a foregone ending. Our "whither," in the widest-ranging sense, outstrips the limits of the factual. No factual account can explain fully, let alone explain away, our basic condition as questioning beings. Questioning as a broad kind of activity is partly an adaptive response to the environment, but the depth of the question "Whither?" exceeds the problems of routine environmental adaptation, crucial though they are. A psychology that claims Heideggerian inspiration will recognize body and mind as intertwining elements in the expansive reality of human being as enworlded pro-jection.

At the same time, Heidegger declines the title of "humanist." He stills the all-too-natural urge to install the human being as the measure of all things in favor of a free recognition of the ineradicably human element in being and knowing combined crucially with a sober respect for, and awe in the face of, the trans-human origin of all being and knowing. Heidegger's human being is at once a mundane reality and a cosmic being. We find ourselves—we experience ourselves in the first instance, and enact meaning throughout our lives—in the diurnal, and our diurnal world rests in the allowance of all that is. At no point may a Heidegger-inspired psychology indulge subjectivism or mere individualism. The human being concerns herself inevitably and essentially with the unique "mine" of her existence, but she ought to do so always with an appreciation of her rootedness in a much greater set of circumstances and with an acceptance of the ineluctably serious responsibility for the chosen character of her life. While answerable for her own life—her ownmost life—the human being is a grant within the broader reality of being. Thus, though her particular choices are truly her own, the need for her to choose—her power of choice itself—is not so. This primal condition calls for humility.

Heidegger also presents us with a complex and challenging vision of truth, and so his understanding of the human condition and the amelioration of experience and identity bears intricate implications. Truth is a-letheia: un/concealing, wherein concealing is equiprimordial with revealing. Untruth is part of truth. An opening supposes a closed zone. As an opening, the human being is a revealing who is imbued nevertheless with murkiness and resistance. This occlusion is not incidental but essential. We are not free to dispense with it. The hiddenness that saturates the human being, who is otherwise a showing, means that we must admit truly our assorted structural limitations. It demands abstemiousness in our ways of knowing and being. As pro-jective or futural and strategic as we are, we find ourselves challenged inescapably by conditions that lie beyond our grasp, we drift away from . . . to fixation on . . . , and the unstoppable nature of death proves our inability to control fully our basic reality. We often know little—we want to know little—about central features of our own intimate reality, though nothing could be closer to us. The otherness, lacunae, drifting, and refusal in human existence are all typal features of the manner in which we dwell in our world. Honesty demands that we acknowledge this truth.

At the same time, and without ultimate contradiction, Heidegger champions the freedom of the human being as a kinetic opening. The opacity of what is closed cannot prevent the revealing of the human being: the constant presence and emergence of the human being in the world, and the human being's interpretive articulatory disclosure, in the widest sense, of what is. The human being is free for . . . , and this freedom is the mark of the human. As an opening, the human being is not a finished being but a project who is underway. Decisions or conditions that hamper the human being's ability to be underway to . . . , to be a project-ion of/into possibilities, constrict his very being in the world. His world of concerns shrinks and degrades. He loses the prospect of fuller appropriative experience and activity. The amelioration of the human condition, therefore, requires a clear devotion to vouchsafing and enriching the human being's capabilities for discovery, revelation, enunciation, decisiveness, and integrity, all in a spirit of honesty and humility. We ought never merely to step in for another—to arrogate a person's process of choice—as this abets existential lethargy and even engenders outright subordination. We ought to step ahead with our fellow sojourner in the quest for a more auspicious understanding of self, others, things, and world. With freedom comes responsibility, and so all the meaning-permeated actions that we decide to undertake—our lives as a whole—are truly ours. Attempts to shrug off this mantle are bound to fail, and at best we can achieve an illusion of freedom without liability. We are called to freedom, but we can be free only through acceptance of the "not" of choice; we find that we are thrown back onto ourselves as we shape our existence through abidance in this meaning but not that one. This is the challenge of the freedom of the human condition, the call to courage.

Becoming authentic, becoming one's "ownmost" person, demands a separation from merely conventional ways of thinking, saying, and acting—from the sphere of the impersonal public in which "every secret loses its force." Packaged intelligibility is fake comprehension, a jumble of glosses that makes faint the call to each Da-sein's unique primal being. When the human being encounters openly and appropriates thoughtfully the factical and projective truths of her existence, she is a self-possessed person. When she does not do so, she is possessed by the indefinite self of "the others." No one—and certainly not the depersonalized and anonymous "one" of the dictum "one ought to think or act thus" that "they" voice—can live her life for her (or die her death for her). Within the encompassing grant of being, she alone is this inescapably localized and individualized receiving-perceiving openness who must respond to the address of what is. *She* is the only *one*. Inhabiting her own(most) possibilities means choosing perseveringly in the face of the distractions and mollifications that the public "they" proffers. The condition of everydayness includes the prospect of transfiguring everydayness.

At the same time, Da-sein finds her orientation, meanings, satisfactions, and happiness among these particular people who fill her world, so the question of how she dwells with others bears a dual nature. While being with others is a risk, it is also indispensable to Da-sein's fulfillment and wholeness. By common account, the deepest contentments and accomplishments of human existence lie in our life together. Furthermore, as we have seen, leaping ahead with the other, rather than leaping for her and thereby diminishing her ability to respond to the address of being, stands as the positive ideal of being with others. When we leap ahead of others to evoke in them a more fitting articulation and appropriation of their basic freedom and meaningful stances, we do them (and even ourselves) the best possible existential service.

As beings in time, we always and already have an understanding of ourselves, others, things, and world. Thus, our understanding is circular in nature: We can begin only where we are. Inspired by Heidegger, we set ourselves the task of interpreting ever more assiduously that with which we are always and already in contact, such as it is. Such interpretation requires respectful attention to what shows itself as it shows itself. This process of understanding unfolds across time; its compass, richness, and wisdom are accomplishments that span the moments of our dwelling.

WORKS CITED

Beauvoir, Simone de. (1964) *The Blood of Others*. London: Penguin Books.

———. (1997) *The Ethics of Ambiguity*. Secaucus, NJ: Citadel Press/Carol Publishing Group.

Beckett, Samuel. (1997) *The Unnamable*. In *Samuel Beckett Trilogy: Molloy, Malone Dies, The Unnamable*, intro. Gabriel Josipovici. New York: Everyman's Library/Alfred Knopf.

Berger, Louis S. (2002) *Psychotherapy as Praxis: Abandoning Misapplied Science*. Victoria, BC: Trafford.

Boss, Medard. (1963) *Psychoanalysis and Daseinsanalysis*, trans. Ludwig B. Lefebre. New York: Basic Books.

———. (1978–1979) "Martin Heidegger's Zollikon Seminars," *Review of Existential Psychology and Psychiatry*, 16:1&2&3, pp. 7–20.

———. (1988) "Recent Considerations in Daseinsanalysis," *The Humanistic Psychologist*, 16:1, pp. 58–74. Special issue: "Psychotherapy for Freedom: The Daseinsanalytic Way in Psychology and Psychoanalysis," guest ed. Erik Craig.

———. (1994) *Existential Foundations of Medicine and Psychology*, trans. Stephen Conway and Anne Cleaves with intro. Paul J. Stern. Northvale, NJ: Jason Aronson Inc.

Brizzi, Monia. (2005) "Heidegger and Joy," *Existential Analysis*, 16:2, pp. 354–369.

Bruns, Gerald L. (1989) *Heidegger's Estrangements: Language, Truth, and Poetry in the Later Writings*. New Haven, CT: Yale University Press.

Clarkson, Petruska. (2004) *Gestalt Counselling in Action*. London: Sage Publications.

Cohn, Hans W. (1997) *Existential Thought and Therapeutic Practice: An Introduction to Existential Psychotherapy*. London: Sage Publications.

———. (1999) "Why Heidegger?", *Existential Analysis*, 10:2, pp. 2–9.

———. (2002) *Heidegger and the Roots of Existential Therapy*. London: Continuum.

Condrau, Gion. (1988) "A Seminar on Daseinsanalytic Psychotherapy," *The Humanistic Psychologist*, 16:1, pp. 101–129. Special issue: "Psychotherapy for Freedom: The Daseinsanalytic Way in Psychology and Psychoanalysis," guest ed. Erik Craig.

Dallmayr, Fred. (1995) "Heidegger and Freud." In *From Phenomenology to Thought, Errancy, and Desire: Essays in Honor of William J. Richardson, S.J.*, ed. Babette E. Babich. Dordrecht: Kluwer, pp. 547–565.

Deurzen, Emmy van. (1999) "Heidegger's Challenge of Authenticity," *Existential Analysis*, 10:1, pp. 115–125.

Deurzen-Smith, Emmy van. (1995) "Heidegger and Psychotherapy," *Existential Analysis*, 6:2, pp. 13–25.

———. (1997). *Everyday Mysteries: Existential Dimensions of Psychotherapy.* Oxford: Routledge.

Dreyfus. Hubert L. (1991) *Being-in-the-World: A Commentary on Heidegger's* Being and Time, *Division I.* Cambridge, MA: MIT Press.

Emad, Parvis. (1991) "The Echo of Being in *Beiträge zur Philosophie—Der Anklang*: Directives for Its Interpretation," *Heidegger Studies*, pp. 15–35.

Frankl, Viktor E. (1967) *Psychotherapy and Existentialism: Selected Papers on Logotherapy.* New York: Touchstone/Simon and Schuster.

Freeman, Kathleen. (1983) *Ancilla to the Pre-Socratic Philosophers: A Complete Translation of the Fragments in Diels,* Fragmente der Vorsokratiker. Cambridge, MA: Harvard University Press.

Frie, Roger, ed. (2003) *Understanding Experience: Psychotherapy and Postmodernism.* Oxford: Routledge.

Gelven, Michael. (1984) "Eros and Projection: Plato and Heidegger." In *Thinking about Being: Aspects of Heidegger's Thought*, ed. Robert W. Shahan and J.N. Mohanty. Norman, OK: University of Oklahoma Press, pp. 125–136.

Gendlin, Eugene T. (1962) *Experiencing and the Creation of Meaning: A Philosophical and Psychological Approach to the Subjective.* Evanston, IL: Northwestern University Press.

———. (1978–1979) "Befindlichkeit: Heidegger and the Philosophy of Psychology," *Review of Existential Psychology and Psychiatry*, 16:1&2&3, pp. 43–71. Available with an addendum at www.focusing.org.

———. (1996) *Focusing-Oriented Psychotherapy: A Manual of the Experiential Method.* New York: The Guilford Press.

Hadot, Pierre. (1995) *Philosophy as a Way of Life: Spiritual Exercises from Socrates to Foucault,* ed. with intro. Arnold I. Davidson and trans. Michael Chase. Oxford: Blackwell.

Hall, Jonathan. (2004) "Understanding and Interpretation in the Clinical Setting: A Heideggerian Perspective," *Existential Analysis*, 15:1, pp. 109–115.

Heidegger, Martin. (1959) *An Introduction to Metaphysics*, trans. Ralph Manheim. New Haven, CT: Yale University Press.

———. (1962) *Being and Time*, trans. John Macquarrie and Edward Robinson. Oxford: Basil Blackwell.

———. (1966a) "Conversation on a Country Path about Thinking." In *Discourse on Thinking: A Translation of* Gelassenheit, trans. John M. Anderson and E. Hans Freund with intro. John M. Anderson. New York: Harper & Row, pp. 58–90.

———. (1966b) "Memorial Address." In *Discourse on Thinking: A Translation of* Gelassenheit, trans. John M. Anderson and E. Hans Freund with intro. John M. Anderson. New York: Harper & Row, pp. 43–57.

———. (1968) *What Is Called Thinking?*, trans. with intro. J. Glenn Gray. New York: Harper & Row.

———. (1971) "Language." In *Poetry, Language, Thought*, trans. with intro. Albert Hofstadter. New York: Harper & Row, pp. 189-210.

———. (1972) "Time and Being." In *On Time and Being*, trans. Joan Stambaugh. New York: Harper Torchbooks, pp. 1–24.

———. (1977a) "On the Essence of Truth." In *Basic Writings*, ed. with gen. intro and section intros. David Farrell Krell. New York: Harper & Row, pp. 117–141.

———. (1977b) "The Question Concerning Technology." In *The Question Concerning Technology and Other Essays*, trans. with intro. William Lovitt. New York: Harper & Row, pp. 3–35.

———. (1988) "On Adequate Understanding of Daseinsanalysis," *The Humanistic Psychologist*, 16:1, pp. 75–98. Special issue: "Psychotherapy for Freedom: The Daseinsanalytic Way in Psychology and Psychoanalysis," guest ed. Erik Craig.

———. (1992) *The Concept of Time*, trans. William McNeil. Oxford: Blackwell.

———. (1995) *The Fundamental Concepts of Metaphysics: World, Finitude, Solitude*, trans. William McNeill and Nicholas Walker. Bloomington, IN: Indiana University Press.

———. (1996) *Being and Time. A Translation of Sein und Zeit*, trans. Joan Stambaugh. Albany, NY: State University of New York Press.

———. (1999) *Contributions to Philosophy (From Enowning)*, trans. Parvis Emad and Kenneth Maly. Bloomington, IN: Indiana University Press.

———. (2001) *Zollikon Seminars: Protocols—Conversations—Letters*, ed. Medard Boss, trans. with notes and afterwords Franz Mayr and Richard Askay. Evanston, IL: Northwestern University Press.

———. (2002) *Identity and Difference*, trans. with intro. Joan Stambaugh. Chicago: University of Chicago Press.

Hersch, Edwin L. (2003) *From Philosophy to Psychotherapy: A Phenomenological Model for Psychology, Psychiatry, and Psychoanalysis.* Toronto: University of Toronto Press.

Hoeller, Keith. (1978–1979) "Introduction," *Review of Existential Psychology and Psychiatry*, 16:1&2&3, pp. 3–6. Special issue: "Heidegger and Psychology," guest ed. Keith Hoeller.

Holmes, Richard. (1995) *The Transcendence of the World: Phenomenological Studies.* Waterloo, ON: Wilfrid Laurier University Press.

Howard, Alex. (2000) *Philosophy for Counselling and Psychotherapy: Pythagoras to Postmodernism.* London: Palgrave.

Jacobsen, Bo. (2003) "Is Gift-Giving the Core of Existential Therapy? A Discussion with Irvin D. Yalom," *Existential Analysis*, 14:2, pp. 345–353.

Kierkegaard, Søren. (1992) *Concluding Unscientific Postscript to* Philosophical Fragments, *Volume I*, ed. and trans. with intro. and notes Howard V. Hong and Edna H. Hong. Princeton, NJ: Princeton University Press.

Kockelmans, Joseph J. (1984) *On the Truth of Being: Reflections on Heidegger's Later Philosophy.* Bloomington, IN: Indiana University Press.

———. (1995) "Reflections on the 'Foundations' of Psychology and Psychoanalysis." In *From Phenomenology to Thought, Errancy, and Desire: Essays in Honor of William J. Richardson, S.J.*, ed. Babette E. Babich. Dordrecht: Kluwer, pp. 527–545.

Kovacs, George. (1992) "The Leap (*der Sprung*) for Being in Heidegger's *Beiträge zur Philosophie (Vom Ereignis)*," *Man and World*, 25:1, pp. 39–59.

Lahav, Ran. (1995) "A Conceptual Framework for Philosophical Counseling: Worldview Interpretation." In *Essays on Philosophical Counseling*, ed. Ran Lahav and Maria da Venza Tillmans. Lanham, MD: University Press of America, pp. 3–24.

Lang, Hermann, Stephan Brunnhuber, and Rudolph Wagner. (2003) "The So-called Zollikon Seminars—Heidegger as a Psychotherapist," *Journal of the American Academy of Psychoanalysis and Dynamic Psychiatry*, 31:2, pp. 349–359.

Lao Tzu. (2000) *Tao Te Ching*, trans. David Hinton. Washington, DC: Counterpoint.

LeBon, Tim. (2001) *Wise Therapy: Philosophy for Counsellors.* London: Continuum.

Levin, David Michael. (1989) *The Listening Self: Personal Growth, Social Change and the Closure of Metaphysics.* Oxford: Routledge.

Mills, Jon. (1997) "The False Dasein: From Heidegger to Sartre and Psychoanalysis," *Journal of Phenomenological Psychology*, 28:1, pp. 42–65.

———. (2002) *The Unconscious Abyss: Hegel's Anticipation of Psychoanalysis.* Albany, NY: State University of New York Press.

———. (2003) "A Phenomenology of Becoming: Reflections of Authenticity." In *Understanding Experience: Psychotherapy and Postmodernism*, ed. Roger Frie. Oxford: Routledge, pp. 116–136.

Nicholson, Graeme. (1986) "Ekstatic Temporality in *Sein und Zeit*." In *A Companion to Martin Heidegger's Being and Time*, ed. Joseph J. Kockelmans. Boca Raton, FL & Lanham, MD: Center for Advanced Research in Phenomenology & University Press of America, pp. 208–226.

Nietzsche, Friedrich. (1982a) "On Truth and Lie in an Extra-Moral Sense." In *The Portable Nietzsche*, sel. and trans. with intro. and notes by Walter Kaufmann. New York: Penguin Books, pp. 42–47.

———. (1982b) *Twilight of the Idols.* In *The Portable Nietzsche*, sel. and trans. with intro. and notes by Walter Kaufmann. New York: Penguin Books, pp. 463–563.

Pessoa, Fernando. (1991) *The Book of Disquiet*, ed. Maria José de Lancastre, trans. Margaret Jull Costa. London: Serpent's Tail.

Rennie, Susanna. (2001) "Fever or Forgotten Wings: The Relevance of Heidegger's Call of Conscience to Psychotherapy," *Existential Analysis*, 12:2, pp. 268–286.

Richardson, William J. (2003) "Truth and Freedom in Psychoanalysis." In *Understanding Experience: Psychotherapy and Postmodernism*, ed. Roger Frie. Oxford: Routledge.

Sallis, John. (1990) *Echoes: After Heidegger.* Bloomington, IN: Indiana University Press.

Sass, Louis A. (1992) "Heidegger, Schizophrenia and the Ontological Difference," *Philosophical Psychology*, 5:2, pp. 109–132.

Schalow, Frank. (1992) "Time as an Afterthought: Differing Views on Imagination," *Philosophy Today*, Spring 1992, pp. 71–82.

Scott, Charles E. (1978–1979) "Psychotherapy: Being One and Many," *Review of Existential Psychology and Psychiatry*, 16:1&2&3, pp. 81–94. Special issue: "Heidegger and Psychology," guest ed. Keith Hoeller.

———. (1990) "Heidegger and Psychoanalysis: The Seminars in *Zollikon*," *Heidegger Studies*, 6, pp. 131–141.

Sheehan, Thomas. (1981) "On Movement and the Destruction of Ontology," *The Monist*, 64:4, pp. 534–542.

———. (2001) "A Paradigm Shift in Heidegger Research," *Continental Philosophy Review*, 34, pp. 183–202.

Spinelli, Ernesto. (1989) *The Interpreted World: An Introduction to Phenomenological Psychology*. London: Sage Publications.

———. (1994) *Demystifying Therapy*. London: Constable.

———. (1997) *Tales of Un-knowing: Therapeutic Encounters from an Existential Perspective*. London: Duckworth.

Thompson, M. Guy. (2004) "Postmodernism and Psychoanalysis: A Heideggerian Critique of Postmodern Malaise and the Question of Authenticity." In *Way Beyond Freud: Postmodern Psychoanalysis Evaluated*, ed. J. Reppen, M. Schulman, and J. Tucker. London: Open Gate Press.

Wilberg, Peter. (2004) *The Therapist as Listener: Martin Heidegger and the Missing Dimension of Counselling and Psychotherapy Training*. New Gnosis Publications, www.newgnosis.co.uk.

Wolf, Darren. (1999) "Heidegger's Conscience," *Existential Analysis*, 10:2, pp. 54–62.

———. (2000) "Everything You Ever Wanted to Know About Heidegger (But Were Afraid to Ask Your Therapist)," *Existential Analysis*, 11:1, pp. 54–62.

Wood, David. (1989) *The Deconstruction of Time*. Atlantic Highlands, NJ: Humanities Press International.

Yalom, Irvin D. (1980) *Existential Psychotherapy*. New York: Basic Books.

ABOUT THE AUTHOR

MARK LETTERI teaches philosophy in Windsor, Ontario, Canada, and hosts an occasional philosophy café and an online philosophical discussion group. He holds a Ph.D. in philosophy from the University of Waterloo, as well as an M.A. in philosophy and a B.A. in psychology from the University of Windsor. Dr. Letteri's scholarly specialization is continental philosophy. His publications and presentations focus on Heidegger, Nietzsche, philosophical practice, reasoning, and educational development. Dr. Letteri oversees scholarly book series in existentialism and the philosophy of psychology. He is also a former first-year studies coordinator and general education teacher, as well as a former test writer and academic managing editor.

INDEX

Absorption, ix, 8, 55, 57, 59, 63–65, 72, 76, 87
Abyss, 39
Action, 4–5, 15, 17–18, 21–22, 27, 40–43, 45, 48, 56, 59, 61–63, 72–73, 75–76, 81–82, 91–93
See also agency
Address, 6, 8, 16, 22–23, 29, 38, 40–41, 47, 50, 52, 56, 60, 89, 93
Adjustment, 29–30, 42, 46
Agency, 4, 43, 59–61
See also action
Aletheia (a-letheia; un/concealing), 6, 18, 38, 57, 70, 74, 76, 92
See also lethe
Ambiguity, 24–26, 29, 55–58, 62, 66, 70–71
Amelioration, 27, 30, 92
Animals, 17, 33, 41, 46, 81–83
Anticipatory care, 40, 85, 88
See also intervening care
Anxiety, 19, 22–23, 66–70
Aphasia, 52
Appropriation, 13, 18, 26, 28, 36, 44, 55, 59, 61–64, 72, 74–77, 80, 85, 87–88, 92–93
See also Ereignis
Aristotle, 4, 36, 81
Articulation, 15, 17, 23, 35, 39–41, 52, 69–70, 76, 85–87, 92–93
Assumptions, 5, 7–8, 34, 47
Attunement, 19, 23–24, 44, 66, 72, 84–85
Authenticity, ix–x, 4, 24, 28, 61–66, 69, 71, 85–86, 89, 93
See also inauthenticity
Autonomy, 80–81
Averageness, 44–45, 56–59, 61, 65, 71–72

Beauvoir, Simone de, 2, 55, 61, 83
Beckett, Samuel, 56
Befindlichkeit, 19–21
Behavior, 17, 25, 42, 82

Behavioral approaches, 83
Being, definition(s) of, 1–2, 13, 71, 73–74, 76–77
See also Sein
Being in the world, 3, 9, 13–18, 21–22, 24, 26–31, 38, 41–43, 46–49, 51–52, 55, 57–66, 69–72, 83–85, 87–89
Being qualities, 44–46, 79, 88
Being t/here, 6, 13–15, 17, 19, 21–23, 25, 29, 33, 35, 38, 46–47, 51–52, 56, 59–60, 63, 67–68, 70, 74, 76, 79, 81, 83–85, 88–89
Being-alongside, 16
Being-for (others), 45, 49, 88
Being-in, 18, 51
Being-toward, 30, 61
Being-with (others), 14, 38, 42–46, 49, 51, 55, 58, 60, 85, 88
See also Mit-sein
Berger, Louis S., 45
Binswanger, Ludwig, 3, 84
Biology, 6, 8, 40, 43, 83, 91
Body, 6–9, 20, 36, 43, 46–52, 63, 80–81, 89, 91
See also bodying forth; corporeality
Bodying forth, 6, 9, 46–47, 49, 51–52, 91
See also body
Boredom, 16, 23–25, 29, 39, 43
Boss, Medard, ix, 3–5, 7, 20–21, 26, 30, 34–35, 37, 43–44, 61, 78, 82, 84–87, 91
Brizzi, Monia, 63, 65–66, 68
Bruns, Gerald L., 76

Calculability, 7, 9, 27, 51–52, 67
Call, 16, 29, 40, 55, 58–59, 61–63, 66, 68, 71–72, 75–76, 82, 85, 87, 89, 92–93
Care, 8–9, 15–18, 25, 27, 29–30, 37, 42–45, 60, 66, 68, 71, 75, 83, 85–86, 88, 92
Causation, 23, 35–36, 40–41

Choice, x, 2–4, 14–15, 21–22, 26, 30, 37, 41, 43, 46, 57, 59–60, 62–65, 67–68, 72, 75, 81, 92–93
Circle of interpretation, 6, 18, 20, 23, 83, 93
 See also hermeneutics; interpretation
Circumspection, 68
Claim (being claimed), 8, 16, 23, 29, 38, 47, 57, 59–61, 63, 72, 84, 87
Clarkson, Petruska, 80
Clearing, 6, 8, 16, 34, 36, 38–39, 52, 60, 63, 77
Client, 9, 21, 26–27, 30, 36, 40, 42, 44–46, 63, 80, 85, 88–89
Clock time, 27, 50
 See also temporality; time
Cognition, 21, 33, 43, 58, 83, 86
Cognitive dissonance, 58
Cognitive approaches, 33, 83, 86
Cohn, Hans W., 16, 18, 36–37, 63–65
Comportment, 8, 21, 27, 34, 44, 47–48, 50, 60–61, 65
Concealing. See un/concealing
Concern. See care
Condition, human. See human condition
Condrau, Gion, 85
Conformism, 58
Connectedness, 43, 50
Conscience, 59, 63, 66–67, 71, 75, 89
Consciousness, 3–5, 15, 20–21, 33–35, 42, 56, 67, 80
Constriction, 29–30, 59, 63, 85, 92
Context, 15, 19–20, 36, 38–41, 58, 63
Contingency, 13, 22
Control, 9, 14, 33, 39, 67, 73, 91–92
Convention, 8, 93
Conversation, 16, 23, 56
Corporeality, 36, 49, 51
 See also body
Cosmos, 5, 34, 38, 58, 80–81, 87
Courage, 93
Curiosity, 55–57, 71

Da, 2, 14, 34, 36, 39, 47
 See also being t/here
Dallmayr, Fred, 37–38

Dasein (Da-sein), definition(s) of, 2, 13–14
Daseinsanalysis, 4, 7–8, 20, 43, 46, 61, 79, 84–87, 91
Death, 4, 27–28, 37, 62–63, 73, 82, 87, 92–93
Decision, 7, 9, 21, 28, 35–37, 40, 45, 48, 55–56, 61–62, 64, 76, 92–93
Depression, 28, 43, 81–82
Depth psychology, 26
Descartes/Cartesianism, 13, 33, 42, 45, 47, 80
Deurzen, Emmy van, ix–x, 42, 63, 66, 68, 79
Deurzen-Smith, Emmy van. See Deurzen, Emmy van
Difference (ontological-ontic), 2, 39, 69
Digression, 57
Disclosing, 1, 19, 22, 24, 36, 42–43, 55–57, 60, 64–66, 69–72, 77, 86, 92
 See also un/concealing
Discourse (discoursing), 58, 66, 71, 75–76, 88
Disowning, ix, 22, 65–66
Dispensability, 57
Dispersion, 55, 57–58
Displacement, 72, 76
Dissociation, 22, 48
Distantiality, 57
Diurnal, 92
Diversion, 64
Doing qualities, 46
Dreyfus, Hubert L., 73
Dwelling, 7–8, 13–15, 17, 25, 27–28, 30, 36, 38, 41–43, 47, 50, 56–57, 70, 72, 74, 76–77, 86–87, 92–94

Ego, 5, 23, 33, 38, 42, 63, 73–74, 81
Eigenwelt, 17
Ek-sistence, 17, 27–29, 51–52, 62–64, 68, 72, 81, 85–86, 88
 See also existence
Ek-static, 15–16, 26–28, 30–31, 38, 51, 57, 60, 76–77, 81, 87
Emad, Parvis, 76

Emergence, 5, 14, 19–20, 30, 39, 41, 51, 63, 65, 68, 70, 79–81, 92
Empathy, 43, 88
Encounter, 6, 16, 21, 41, 52, 55, 60–61, 66, 80, 83, 88, 93
Enframing, 73
Engagement, ix, 16–17, 20–21, 26–27, 29, 45, 51, 58, 60, 66, 86–88
Entwurf, 18, 43, 46, 71–72, 74, 76
　See also projection
Environment, 9, 17, 41, 91
Enworldment, 14–15, 17, 21, 23, 25, 41, 49, 58–59, 68, 70, 76, 81, 91
Ereignis (event of appropriation), 74–77
　See also appropriation
Ethics, 87
Everydayness, 17, 20, 28–29, 44, 49, 55–59, 61, 65, 67–68, 70–72, 76, 85, 93
Existence, ix, 2, 4, 8, 14, 17, 19, 23, 33, 37, 40, 42, 47, 50, 55, 58–59, 61, 63, 66–69, 71–73, 75, 80–82, 85, 92–93
　See also ek-sistence
Existential, ix, 1–4, 16–17, 22, 35–37, 41–44, 46, 57, 61–65, 68, 70, 75, 79, 81–82, 85–86, 88, 93
Experience (experiencing), 2, 6–8, 15, 17, 19–22, 24–26, 33, 36, 39, 41, 45–46, 50, 52, 57, 67, 69, 72, 74, 76, 79–81, 86–89, 92

Falling (fallenness), 44, 55, 57–58, 61–62, 64, 66, 68
Fear, 22, 59, 70
Felt sense, 19–20, 22–23
Festinger, Leon, 58
Figure, 50, 62, 79–80
Finding, 13, 16–17, 19–23, 30, 33–34, 63–64, 70, 91–93
Finitude, 23, 63, 68, 77
Forgetting, 9, 21, 35, 37–38, 55, 61, 69–70, 87
Frankl, Viktor E., 81–83
Freedom, 14, 24–25, 29–30, 35, 37–40, 47, 58–60, 62–65, 67–68, 70, 81–82, 84–88, 91–93

Freeman, Kathleen, 77
Freud, Sigmund, 22, 25–26, 35, 37–40, 82, 84
Frie, Roger, 3
Future, 14, 22, 26–31, 46, 50–51, 72, 81, 85, 92

Galileo, 47
Gathering together, 18, 27, 48, 61, 72, 76–77
Gelassenheit, 71, 74
　See also releasement
Gelven, Michael, 75
Gendlin, Eugene T., 19–21, 48, 79
Gestalt, 24, 39, 50, 79–81
Gesture (bodily), 48–49
Geworfenheit, 26, 72, 74, 76
　See also thrownness
Given, 6, 36, 50, 63–64, 83
Giving, 74–77, 80–81
Goals (therapeutic), 29, 66, 84
Ground, 2, 5, 40–41, 46–47, 50–51, 56, 58, 62, 67, 71, 79–80
Guilt, 67–68

Hadot, Pierre, 10
Hall, Jonathan, 14, 17, 66
Hearing. *See* listening
Hegel, G.W.F., 39–40
Heraclitus, 70, 77
Here, 13–15, 27, 46, 51, 56, 59
　See also being t/here
Hermeneutics, 4, 6, 17–23, 26, 35, 47, 49, 51, 57, 63, 83, 91
　See also circle of interpretation
Hersch, Edwin L., 15, 18, 48, 84
Hiddenness, 15, 31, 34, 44, 92
History, 3, 5, 21, 25–27, 29–30, 38–39, 56, 60–61, 72, 76, 83
Hoeller, Keith, 3
Holism, 9, 48, 83
Holmes, Richard, 6, 26
Honesty, 92
Howard, Alex, 45
Human condition, 3–4, 8, 14–16, 22, 25, 28, 44, 58, 71, 76, 86–87, 91–93
Humanism, 3–4, 79–81, 91

Humility, 81, 92
Husserl, Edmund, 4–5, 7, 20–21, 80

Identity 16, 24, 35, 39, 57–58, 60–61, 74, 92
Idle talk, 55–57, 75
Illness, 30, 42, 59, 64
Inauthenticity, ix, 23–24, 27, 42, 48
    See also authenticity
Indifference, 23
Individual, 2, 4, 17, 28–30, 39, 42–44, 58, 63, 71, 83, 85, 92–93
Individuation, 43, 58
Intentionality, x, 37
Interpretation, 4–7, 9, 14–15, 18, 20, 22–24, 26, 29, 33, 36–38, 40, 42–43, 46, 52, 57, 62, 70, 72, 81, 83, 87, 91–93
    See also circle of interpretation
Interrogation, 13, 58, 73, 81, 91
Intervening care, 40, 85, 88
    See also anticipatory care
Invisible. See visible
Involvement, 16, 21, 37
Irresoluteness, 21

Jacobsen, Bo, 86
Jaspers, Karl, 5

Kant, Immanuel (Kantianism), 25, 73
Kierkegaard, Søren, 2, 4, 57, 62, 68, 70
Kinesis, 15, 27, 29, 34, 38–39, 58–60, 92
Knowledge (knowing), 1, 9, 19, 24, 28, 34, 36, 55–57, 59, 62, 66–67, 69, 72, 74, 80, 86, 91–92
Kockelmans, Joseph J., 3, 8, 20, 38, 74, 87
Kovacs, George, 76

Lacan, Jacques, 38, 56
Lack, 16, 23–24, 40, 43, 52, 55, 68–69, 82
Lahav, Ran, 17
Lang, Hermann, Stephan Brunnhuber, and Rudolph Wagner, 35, 39, 43

Language, 1, 4–5, 9, 14–15, 17, 34–35, 41, 52, 57, 75, 84, 88–89
    See also saying
Lao Tzu, 74
Leaping ahead, 5, 84–86, 88, 93
    See also leaping for
Leaping for, 85, 88, 93
    See also leaping ahead
LeBon, Tim, 15
Lethe (concealing), 6, 18, 38, 57, 70, 74, 76, 92
    See also aletheia
Levelling (down), 55, 57–58
Levin, David Michael, 73
Listening, 8–9, 24, 35, 39–40, 43, 45, 48, 63, 68, 73, 76, 88–89
Lived world, 4, 17, 27, 45, 50, 80, 88, 91
Localization, 14, 24, 58, 81, 83, 93
Logic, 7
Logos, 7, 83
Logotherapy, 81–83

Madness, 42, 76
Manageability, 27, 67, 91
Matter of thinking, 2, 7, 13, 19, 26, 72–73, 75–76
    See also thinking
Meaning, 6–7, 13–15, 17, 23, 26, 28, 30–31, 36–37, 42–44, 46–49, 51–52, 56, 59–60, 62, 66–67, 70, 72–73, 75, 79–83, 87–89, 92–93
Measurability, 8–9, 27, 33, 35, 48–50
Medicine, 3, 8, 64, 85
Meditative thinking, 4, 26, 34–35, 63, 73
Memory, 44, 51
Merleau-Ponty, Maurice, 6, 8
Metaphysics, 1, 3, 69, 73, 79, 81, 83
Method, 5, 9, 36, 51, 71, 87
Mills, Jon, 4, 39–40, 62, 65–66, 85
Mind, 7–8, 22, 37, 44, 81, 91
Mindfulness, 89
Mineness, x, 59–60, 63–64, 75, 92
Mit-sein, 44, 88
    See also being-with
Mitwelt, 17

Mood, 19–20, 24, 74
   See also Stimmung
Mortality, 2, 13, 23, 25, 29, 87
Motive, 15, 23, 36, 40–41
Mystery, 26, 34, 39, 59, 67, 73–74, 77

Narcissism, 4, 7
Natural science. *See* science
Naturalism, 22, 47–49
Neurosis, 61, 69–70
Nicholson, Graeme, 72–76
Nietzsche, Friedrich, 2–4, 22, 26, 43, 73, 82–83
Nihilism, 71
Noetic, 81–82, 91
Not, 60, 67–68, 93
Nothing, 21–24, 56, 70
Now, 14, 21, 26–27, 37, 50, 61, 66
Nullity, 43, 67–68

Objectivity, 14, 18, 47, 62, 69, 82–83
Objects, 5–9, 13–16, 18, 22, 33, 42–45, 47, 49, 51–52, 69, 73, 75, 86–87, 91
Occlusion, 38–39, 56, 80, 92
Ontic, ix, 1, 66, 69, 75
   See also difference
Ontological exposure, 38, 68
Ontological, ix, 1–2, 4–8, 38–39, 63, 66, 68–74, 76–77, 81, 87, 91
   See also difference; ontological exposure
Opacity, 18, 23, 39, 66, 77, 92
Openness, 2, 5–9, 14–16, 18, 20–23, 27, 29, 34, 36, 38, 40–42, 47–52, 55, 58–63, 66, 68, 70–77, 79–80, 82–87, 89, 91–93
Operationalization, 8
Organism, 6, 22, 48, 80–83
Orientation, 9, 15, 19, 41, 47–48, 60–61, 72, 76, 93
Ownmostness, x, 22, 27–30, 55, 57, 59, 64–66, 68, 85, 87–88, 92–93

Paradoxical intention, 82
Past, 14, 21, 25–31, 37, 50–51, 67, 72, 75
Pathology. *See* psychopathology

Perseverance, 45, 88, 93
Pessoa, Fernando, 48
Phenomena, 5–9, 19, 22–28, 34–37, 41–42, 47–51, 56–58, 62, 67, 69–70, 79, 81–82, 84, 87
Phenomenology, 4, 7–9, 17–18, 20–22, 26, 36, 44, 47–51, 71, 73, 79–80, 86, 88
Play, 80–81
Possibility, 8–9, 13–14, 16–19, 21–23, 25–29, 34, 43–44, 46, 49, 51, 55, 57, 59–67, 70–75, 77, 83–89, 92–93
Postmodernism, 4, 23, 38–39, 71
Preoccupation, x, 30, 81
Pres-ab-sential bivalence, 38, 73
Presence, 18, 30, 33, 37–38, 41, 43, 51–52, 69, 74, 87, 89, 92
Present (time), 14, 21, 26–31, 37, 50–51, 72
Present-to-hand (present-at-hand), 5, 16, 18, 34, 66
   See also ready-to-hand
Pre-understanding, 20
   See also understanding
Process, 17, 19–20, 22, 27–28, 36, 38–40, 56, 62, 69, 73, 79–80, 87, 89, 93–94
Progress, 58, 68
Projection (pro-jection), 14–18, 22, 26, 29–30, 40–43, 46–52, 60, 63–64, 67–68, 71–77, 81, 85, 88, 91–93
   See also Entwurf
"Psy" phenomena, 4, 9, 70, 91
Psyche, 5, 7–8, 25, 34, 48
Psychiatry, 3, 5, 7, 87
Psychoanalysis, 26, 30, 35, 37, 39, 79, 84, 87
Psychology, 1, 3–5, 7, 9, 21–22, 24, 26, 29, 34–35, 37–38, 40, 44, 50, 65, 70, 79–82, 84, 87, 91–92
Psychopathology, x, 5, 29, 34, 42, 69, 84
Psychosis, 69–70
Psychotherapy, ix, 1–4, 9, 20–21, 25–27, 29–30, 35–37, 42, 44–46, 62, 66–67, 69, 79–89

Quantity, 27, 37–38, 49
Questioning, 1–2, 7, 9, 15, 21, 23, 26, 31, 34, 39, 47, 59, 71–74, 76, 81, 85–87, 91

Rationalization, 22
Ready-to-hand, 18, 66
  See also present-to-hand
Reality, 4–9, 14–15, 17–19, 21–23, 25–26, 28–29, 33–34, 37–39, 41–42, 44–45, 47, 51–52, 55–58, 60, 62, 64, 69–73, 76–77, 81, 83, 87–89, 91–92
Reason, 22
  See also rationality
Rationality, 59, 81
  See also reason
Receiving-perceiving, 5–6, 9, 16, 21–23, 33, 38, 42–43, 47–48, 50–52, 60, 69, 72, 84–85, 87, 93
Receptivity, 16, 45, 88
Recollection, 1, 21, 63, 72–73
Reductionism, 4, 8, 22, 79, 83
Reflection, 7, 9, 17, 19, 50, 71, 74, 82, 87–89
Reflexivity, 39, 63, 82
Refusal, 24–25, 45, 55–56, 92
Regional ontology, 5, 24, 87
Relationality, 9, 15, 17–18, 21, 27, 33, 35–36, 41–46, 48–49, 51, 60–61, 65, 70, 77, 86, 88
Releasement, 71–77
  See also Gelassenheit
Remembering, 36, 51
Rennie, Susanna, 89
Representation, 5, 36, 41, 73–74
Resoluteness, 21, 42–43, 62, 68, 85
Responsibility, 2, 4, 14, 28, 39–40, 55, 60, 67, 80, 85, 92–93
Responsiveness, 6, 38, 63, 74, 84–85, 87
Reticence, 39, 55, 71, 75
Richardson, William J., 37–39, 56–57, 71, 84, 86
Rigor, 5, 9

Sallis, John, 75

Sartre, Jean-Paul, 2, 8, 48, 65, 67, 70, 79
Sass, Louis A., 68–70
Saying, 15, 35, 76, 93
  See also language
Schalow, Frank, 77
Schizophrenia, 68–69
Science, 2, 4–9, 21, 33–37, 41, 45, 47–49, 51–52, 87–88, 91
Scott, Charles E., 73, 84
Sedimentation, 59
Sein, 1–2
  See also being
Self, ix, 4–5, 16, 20–21, 24, 33, 38, 41–42, 55–65, 67, 69, 71–73, 76–77, 81, 93
Self-exiting, 72, 76
Sheehan, Thomas, 1–2, 7, 14, 18–19, 38, 68, 73, 76–77
Showing, 6, 39, 52, 88, 92, 94
Silence, 19, 66, 71, 75, 88–89
Situatedness. *See* situation
Situation, 7, 15, 19, 21, 36, 47, 49–50, 59–60, 68, 72, 82, 89
Social science, 5–6, 8–9
Sojourning, 7, 13, 16, 21, 28–30, 34, 46, 48, 50–51, 55, 60–61, 63, 87, 93
Somatic, 7–8, 47, 81
Spatiality, 8, 15, 21, 34, 46–51, 63, 75
Span (spanning), 15, 24, 50–51, 94
Spinelli, Ernesto, 44–46, 59, 72, 79, 88–89
Standing out, 59
Stimmung, 19
  See also mood
Stress, 16–17, 22–23, 27, 29, 41
Subject (subjectivity), 2–5, 7, 21, 42–43, 51, 60, 62, 69, 71–73, 75, 81, 83–84, 92
Substance, 16, 60
Summoning, 59, 61, 66, 71, 89
Symptoms, 27, 37, 88

Talking cure, 35, 40, 84, 88
Technical, 7, 27, 33, 35, 44–45, 58, 67, 84, 86
Technique, 8, 46, 82, 84, 89

Index 109

Technology, 57, 73
Temporality, 15–16, 24–31, 34, 43, 50, 61–62, 72, 75–76
 See also time
Thematization, 19, 50, 87
Theory, 1, 4, 7–9, 20, 33, 35, 44, 59, 86–88
Therapeutic goals. *See* goals
Therapy. *See* psychotherapy
T/here. *See* being t/here; here
"They," 55–59, 63, 65, 67, 71, 75, 93
Things, 6–8, 13, 15–16, 18, 20, 22–25, 33–37, 39, 41, 47–49, 51–52, 55, 60–61, 70–71, 73–74, 77, 80, 83–87, 91, 93
Thinking, 2–4, 7, 9, 19, 26, 35, 39, 41, 48, 55, 69, 71–77, 80–81, 91
 See also matter of thinking
Thompson, M. Guy, 5, 38, 66
Thrownness, 14–15, 17–18, 26, 28, 37, 46, 60, 63, 68, 72, 74, 76, 85–86, 93
 See also Geworfenheit
Time, 7, 14–16, 21, 23–31, 46, 49–51, 55, 68, 74–76, 87, 93–94
 See also temporality
Transcendence, ix, 8, 21, 58, 60, 73, 75, 80, 83, 88
Triviality, 57–58, 71
Truth, 4–6, 14–15, 17, 21–23, 25, 28, 33, 38, 40, 42–43, 45, 48–49, 55–57, 59, 62, 66–67, 69–72, 74, 76–77, 80–81, 84, 86–88, 92–93
 See also untruth
Turbulence, 61
Turn, 2

Umwelt, 17
Uncanniness, 19, 22, 63, 68, 72, 75–77, 81
Un/concealing, 6, 26, 29–30, 34, 36, 38–40, 52, 55–56, 70–71, 73–74, 80–81, 84, 86–87, 89, 92
 See also disclosing
Understanding, 6, 8, 15, 17–22, 26, 30, 36, 41–42, 46–47, 49, 52, 55, 57–58, 62, 64–65, 72–73, 75–76, 83–85, 87–88, 93
 See also pre-understanding
Unhomelikeness, 72
Untruth, 38, 70, 92
 See also truth

Vernehmen, 5
Vibrancy, 29
Visible, 5–6, 52, 66
 See also invisible

Wholeness, 34, 41, 65, 74, 83, 93
Who-ness, 35, 39
Wilberg, Peter, 63, 88–89
Willing, 61, 74–75
Wisdom, 57, 94
Withdrawal, 6, 24–25, 38–39, 73–74, 80
Wolf, Darren, 9, 67, 71, 89
Wood, David, 75
World, 3–4, 6, 8–10, 13–30, 33, 36, 38–43, 45–52, 55–60, 62–65, 67, 69–72, 74, 76–77, 80–88, 91–93

Yalom, Irvin D., 1, 86

VIBS

The **Value Inquiry Book Series** is co-sponsored by:

Adler School of Professional Psychology
American Indian Philosophy Association
American Maritain Association
American Society for Value Inquiry
Association for Process Philosophy of Education
Canadian Society for Philosophical Practice
Center for Bioethics, University of Turku
Center for Professional and Applied Ethics, University of North Carolina at Charlotte
Central European Pragmatist Forum
Centre for Applied Ethics, Hong Kong Baptist University
Centre for Cultural Research, Aarhus University
Centre for Professional Ethics, University of Central Lancashire
Centre for the Study of Philosophy and Religion, University College of Cape Breton
Centro de Estudos em Filosofia Americana, Brazil
College of Education and Allied Professions, Bowling Green State University
College of Liberal Arts, Rochester Institute of Technology
Concerned Philosophers for Peace
Conference of Philosophical Societies
Department of Moral and Social Philosophy, University of Helsinki
Gannon University
Gilson Society
Haitian Studies Association
Ikeda University
Institute of Philosophy of the High Council of Scientific Research, Spain
International Academy of Philosophy of the Principality of Liechtenstein
International Association of Bioethics
International Center for the Arts, Humanities, and Value Inquiry
International Society for Universal Dialogue
Natural Law Society
Philosophical Society of Finland
Philosophy Born of Struggle Association
Philosophy Seminar, University of Mainz
Pragmatism Archive at The Oklahoma State University
R.S. Hartman Institute for Formal and Applied Axiology
Research Institute, Lakeridge Health Corporation
Russian Philosophical Society
Society for Existential Analysis
Society for Iberian and Latin-American Thought
Society for the Philosophic Study of Genocide and the Holocaust
Unit for Research in Cognitive Neuroscience, Autonomous University of Barcelona
Yves R. Simon Institute

Titles Published

Volumes 1 - 162 see www.rodopi.nl

163. Reyes Mate, *Memory of the West: The Contemporaneity of Forgotten Jewish Thinkers.* Translated from the Spanish by Anne Day Dewey. Edited by John R. Welch. A volume in **Philosophy in Spain**

164. Nancy Nyquist Potter, Editor, *Putting Peace into Practice: Evaluating Policy on Local and Global Levels.* A volume in **Philosophy of Peace**

165. Matti Häyry, Tuija Takala, and Peter Herissone-Kelly, Editors, *Bioethics and Social Reality.* A volume in **Values in Bioethics**

166. Maureen Sie, *Justifying Blame: Why Free Will Matters and Why it Does Not.* A volume in **Studies in Applied Ethics**

167. Leszek Koczanowicz and Beth J. Singer, Editors, *Democracy and the Post-Totalitarian Experience.* A volume in **Studies in Pragmatism and Values**

168. Michael W. Riley, *Plato's* Cratylus: *Argument, Form, and Structure.* A volume in **Studies in the History of Western Philosophy**

169. Leon Pomeroy, *The New Science of Axiological Psychology.* Edited by Rem B. Edwards. A volume in **Hartman Institute Axiology Studies**

170. Eric Wolf Fried, *Inwardness and Morality*

171. Sami Pihlstrom, *Pragmatic Moral Realism: A Transcendental Defense.* A volume in Studies in **Pragmatism and Values**

172. Charles C. Hinkley II, *Moral Conflicts of Organ Retrieval: A Case for Constructive Pluralism.* A volume in **Values in Bioethics**

173. Gábor Forrai and George Kampis, Editors, *Intentionality: Past and Future.* A volume in **Cognitive Science**

174. Dixie Lee Harris, *Encounters in My Travels: Thoughts Along the Way.* A volume in **Lived Values:Valued Lives**

175. Lynda Burns, Editor, *Feminist Alliances.* A volume in **Philosophy and Women**

176.   George Allan and Malcolm D. Evans, *A Different Three Rs for Education*. A volume in **Philosophy of Education**

177.   Robert A. Delfino, Editor, *What are We to Understand Gracia to Mean?: Realist Challenges to Metaphysical Neutralism*. A volume in **Gilson Studies**

178.   Constantin V. Ponomareff and Kenneth A. Bryson, *The Curve of the Sacred: An Exploration of Human Spirituality*. A volume in **Philosophy and Religion**

179.   John Ryder, Gert Rüdiger Wegmarshaus, Editors, *Education for a Democratic Society: Central European Pragmatist Forum, Volume Three*. A volume in **Studies in Pragmatism and Values**

180.   Florencia Luna, *Bioethics and Vulnerability: A Latin American View*. A volume in **Values in Bioethics**

181.   John Kultgen and Mary Lenzi, Editors, *Problems for Democracy*. A volume in **Philosophy of Peace**

182.   David Boersema and Katy Gray Brown, Editors, *Spiritual and Political Dimensions of Nonviolence and Peace*. A volume in **Philosophy of Peace**

183.   Daniel P. Thero, *Understanding Moral Weakness*. A volume in **Studies in the History of Western Philosophy**

184.   Scott Gelfand and John R. Shook, Editors, *Ectogenesis: Artificial Womb Technology and the Future of Human Reproduction*. A volume in **Values in Bioethics**

185.   Piotr Jaroszyński, *Science in Culture*. A volume in **Gilson Studies**

186.   Matti Häyry, Tuija Takala, Peter Herissone-Kelly, Editors, *Ethics in Biomedical Research: International Perspectives*. A volume in **Values in Bioethics**

187.   Michael Krausz, *Interpretation and Transformation: Explorations in Art and the Self*. A volume in **Interpretation and Translation**

188.   Gail M. Presbey, Editor, *Philosophical Perspectives on the "War on Terrorism."* A volume in **Philosophy of Peace**

189. María Luisa Femenías, Amy A. Oliver, Editors, *Feminist Philosophy in Latin America and Spain*. A volume in **Philosophy in Latin America**

190. Oscar Vilarroya and Francesc Forn I Argimon, Editors, *Social Brain Matters: Stances on the Neurobiology of Social Cognition*. A volume in **Cognitive Science**

191. Eugenio Garin, *History of Italian Philosophy*. Translated from Italian and Edited by Giorgio Pinton. A volume in **Values in Italian Philosophy**

192. Michael Taylor, Helmut Schreier, and Paulo Ghiraldelli, Jr., Editors, *Pragmatism, Education, and Children: International Philosophical Perspectives*. A volume in **Pragmatism and Values**

193. Brendan Sweetman, *The Vision of Gabriel Marcel: Epistemology, Human Person, the Transcendent*. A volume in **Philosophy and Religion**

194. Danielle Poe and Eddy Souffrant, Editors, *Parceling the Globe: Philosophical Explorations in Globalization, Global Behavior, and Peace*. A volume in **Philosophy of Peace**

195. Josef Šmajs, *Evolutionary Ontology: Reclaiming the Value of Nature by Transforming Culture*. A volume in **Central-European Value Studies**

196. Giuseppe Vicari, *Beyond Conceptual Dualism: Ontology of Consciousness, Mental Causation, and Holism in John R. Searle's Philosophy of Mind.* **A volume in Cognitive Science**

197. Avi Sagi, *Tradition vs. Traditionalism: Contemporary Perspectives in Jewish Thought*. Translated from Hebrew by Batya Stein. A volume in **Philosophy and Religion**

198. Randall E. Osborne and Paul Kriese, Editors, *Global Community: Global Security*. A volume in **Studies in Jurisprudence**

199. Craig Clifford, *Learned Ignorance in the Medicine Bow Mountains: A Reflection on Intellectual Prejudice.* A volume in **Lived Values: Valued Lives**

200. Mark Letteri, *Heidegger and the Question of Psychology: Zollikon and Beyond*. A volume in **Philosophy and Psychology**

www.ingramcontent.com/pod-product-compliance
Lightning Source LLC
Chambersburg PA
CBHW030117010526
44116CB00005B/280